SO-AQM-716

Essential
Turkey
South Coast

by Melissa Shales

Melissa Shales is a freelance writer and editor who has been travelling since the age of four and writing about travel since the age of 22. She is the author of over a dozen travel guides, including several for the AA (on Kenya, South Africa, Delhi and Rajasthan and France) and amongst various editing jobs was Series Adviser on the AA/Thomas Cook Traveller Guides and editor of *Traveller* magazine.

Above: *watersports off Kemer beach*

AA Publishing

Above: *boat trips are a good way of seeing the cliff-top citadel of Alanya*

Front cover: *Alanya harbour; a gület; Antalya; woman in traditional costume*

Written by Melissa Shales

Produced by AA Publishing.
© The Automobile Association 1999
Maps © The Automobile Association 1999
Reprinted Nov 1999
Reprinted May 2001

Distributed in the United Kingdom by AA Publishing, Norfolk House, Priestley Road, Basingstoke, Hampshire, RG24 9NY.

A CIP catalogue record for this book is available from the British Library.

ISBN 0 7495 1923 1

Published by AA Publishing, a trading name of Automobile Association Developments Limited, whose registered office is Norfolk House, Priestley Road, Basingstoke, Hampshire, RG24 9NY.
Registered number 1878835.

Colour separation: Pace Colour, Southampton
Printed and bound in Italy by Printer Trento srl

Find out more about AA Publishing and the wide range of services the AA provides by visiting our web site at www.theaa.co.uk

Contents

About this Book

Essential *Turkey South Coast* is divided into five sections to cover the most important aspects of your visit to the area.

Viewing Southern Turkey pages 5–14
An introduction to the area by the author.
  Southern Turkey's Features
  Essence of Southern Turkey
  The Shaping of Southern Turkey
  Peace and Quiet
  Southern Turkey's Famous

Top Ten pages 15–26
The author's choice of the Top Ten places to see in the area, in alphabetical order, each with practical information.

What to See pages 27–92
Three sections covering the main areas of the Turkish South Coast, each with its own brief introduction and an alphabetical listing of the main attractions.
  Practical information
  Snippets of 'Did You Know...' information
  2 suggested walks
  4 suggested drives/cruises
  2 features

Where To... pages 93–116
Detailed listings of the best places to eat, stay, shop, take the children and be entertained.

Practical Matters pages 117–24
A highly visual section containing essential travel information.

Maps
All map references are to the individual map found in the What to See section of this guide.
For example, Olympos and the Chimaera have the reference ✚ 28B1 – indicating the page on which the map is located and the grid square in which the sights are to be found. A list of maps that have been used in this travel guide can be found in the index.

Prices
Where appropriate, an indication of the cost of an establishment is given by **£** signs:
£££ denotes higher prices, **££** denotes average prices, while **£** denotes lower prices.

Star Ratings
Most of the places described in this book have been given a separate rating:

✪✪✪ Do not miss
✪✪ Highly recommended
✪ Worth seeing

4

Viewing
Southern
Turkey

Above: *the Kızıl Kule (Red Tower) guards Alanya harbour*
Right: *itinerant tea seller in Adana*

Melissa Shales's Southern Turkey

When to Go

The winters are generally mild, but often surprisingly grey and wet; mid-summer is often desperately hot and dry, with temperatures reaching 45°C at midday. Ideally, the best time to visit the area is in April and May, when the daytime temperature is a pleasant 25°C, the evenings are still sufficiently balmy to sit outdoors and the hills are vibrant with spring flowers. In spite of this, the official tourist season doesn't start until mid-May.

Turkey is glorious, complicated, invigorating, confusing, refreshing, sometimes annoying and always utterly fascinating, with at least three entirely separate identities. First there is tourist Turkey, a wafer-thin veneer of expensive shops, shiny new hotels, topless bathing, beer gardens and far too much development. Next is Westernised Turkey, the reality for many Turks who have grown up in the cities or along the coast, living a European lifestyle with Islam somewhere in the background and MTV well to the fore. And then there is traditional Turkey. Head inland a couple of miles, or turn the corner into the poorer backstreets and there are the women in baggy trousers, cardigans and scarves, the men with hubble-bubble pipes and backgammon boards. Every road has a pothole and a hairpin bend, every house is either half-built or falling down. Hospitality, friendship and the blood feud co-exist.

Finally, as if modern Turkey wasn't complicated enough, add around 8,000 years of history, the wonderful mountain scenery, an impossibly turquoise sea, the baking sun, shaggy black and gold goats, olive groves and apple blossom, pine trees and wild thyme.

To me, this is a dream destination, with exactly the right mix of warmth, friendship and curiosity, history and beauty, and a rather anarchic attitude towards efficiency. I was astonished by the beauty of Lycia, loved the cities of Antalya and Alanya and, to my amazement, found the eastern section of the coast, with its echoes of the Bible and the Crusades and its entirely Asian lifestyle, most fascinating of all.

View from the citadel over Alanya harbour and the 13th-century Kızıl Kule (Red Tower)

Southern Turkey's Features

- Anatolia (based on a Greek word meaning 'east') is the term used to describe the vast mass of Asian Turkey, as opposed to the tiny corner in the northwest (Thrace) that is officially part of Europe. The Romans referred to Anatolia as Asia Minor.

- Turkey has a population of about 60 million, of whom about 98 per cent are Muslim.

- The original Turks were descended from the fiercely combative nomadic Tukin people, from the same high plains of central Asia as the Mongols. Genghis Khan was half-Turkish.

- Turkish belongs to the Ural-Altaic group of languages, together with Finnish and Hungarian, Japanese, Korean and – possibly – Navaho.

- Not only did Atatürk create modern Turkey (➤ 11), along the way he converted the language to the Western alphabet, and banned the fez and turban as symbols of officialdom, and women's veils as symbols of oppression. He is revered today, with his portrait in every building and his statue in every town.

- Turkey's most famous folk hero is Nasreddin Hodja, a teacher and magistrate who died in 1284. A sort of combination of Oscar Wilde and Aesop, he was a wise wit who coined many famous epigrams. Stories continue to be woven around him, in film, cartoon, on paper and through folk tradition.

Crescent beaches along the Mediterranean coast of Anamur

- Turkey covers 814,578sq km, and two continents, with the Bosphorus in Istanbul dividing Europe and Asia. The country is bordered by seven countries and four seas – the Mediterranean, the Aegean, the Sea of Marmara and the Black Sea – with a coastline over 8,333km long. The Mediterranean coast is 1,577km long.

Essence of Southern Turkey

Right: *painted dolls made from gourds are a speciality of Pamphylia*

Below: *a drink, a view and the late afternoon sun on Fethiye*

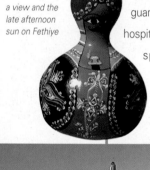

For 2,000 years, Turkey's Mediterranean coast was the hub of the known world. For the next 1,500, it faded into obscurity, its startlingly beautiful coast inhabited only by goats and fishermen. Today, it is experiencing a huge and rapid revival as one of the great tourist centres of the world, offering a compulsive mix of guaranteed sunshine, warm, turquoise water, hospitality, good food, a wealth of history and spectacular mountainscapes. Out of season, almost the entire coast is a building site, in season a bazaar. All year round, it is enchanting.

THE 10 ESSENTIALS

*If you only have a short time to visit,
or would like to get a really complete picture of
the country, here are the essentials:*

- **Drift along** past cliffs and caves, stretched out on the wooden deck of a *gület* (traditional boat), listening to the lapping of the gentle Mediterranean waves.
- **Sit at a harbour-front restaurant** eating steaming *calamari* and sun-drenched tomato salad, washed down with orange juice fresh from the tree.
- **Hike through the pine forests** and across mountains strewn with flowers, breathing in the scent of wild thyme and oregano, and then collapse with pleasant exhaustion on the walls of a ruined mountain-top city or castle.
- **Sip a glass of çay (tea)** as jewel-coloured carpets made from wool and silk pile around your feet and you get down to some serious haggling.
- **Stand centre stage at Aspendos** and proclaim to the ghosts of emperors in a theatre that has been used for over 2,000 years (➤ 18).
- **Stretch out on the sand** and spend a day working on the ultimate tan.
- **Squat on a dusty village track** talking to the local women and children and a flock of golden-fleeced sheep through mime and drawings, sharing their *börek* (➤ 50) and your chocolate.
- **Lie face-down on a marble slab** in a colonnaded steam room and let a vigorous masseur or masseuse release the kinks from your muscles and the grime from your pores in a Turkish bath.
- **Gasp at the antiquity of the area** as you visit the places where Mark Anthony met Cleopatra (➤ 90), where saints Peter, Paul and Barnabas decided to call their new church 'Christian' (➤ 80), or where the god Apollo was said to spend his winter holiday (➤ 68).
- **Party under the stars** until the early hours of the morning at a waterfront open-air disco, cooled by a brisk sea breeze.

Above: *serious retail therapy – carpet shopping is an art form in itself*

Below: *shrug off the cares of the day with a massage at the local hamam (Turkish bath)*

The Shaping of
Southern Turkey

c6500–5400 BC
The city of Çatalhöyük
(► 89) is established –
the world's second
oldest, after Jericho.

c1900–1150 BC
Golden era of the Hittite
Empire, an advanced
civilisation contemporary
with Babylon and ancient
Egypt (► 20).

from c1250 BC
Successive invaders set
up new kingdoms, includ-
ing the powerful Phrygian
civilisation, ruled by legen-
dary kings such as Midas
(in the 8th century BC).

Below: *St Paul preaching a
sermon at Ephesus*

c650 BC
The Phrygian Empire is
destroyed by Lydians,
whose most famous king
was Croesus. Other
Greek states developing
along the coast include
Lycia, Pamphylia and
Cilicia.

546 BC
Cyrus of Persia conquers
Anatolia, which remains
under Persian rule for
nearly 200 years.

334–23 BC
Alexander the Great
sweeps across Anatolia,
reconquering all former
Greek territories.

4th–2nd centuries BC
Seleucids and Ptolemies
compete for control of
the Greek territories
along the coast.

133 BC
Romans begin conquest
of Anatolia, renaming it
Asia Minor.

AD 45–58
St Paul the Evangelist
travels and preaches
widely along the coast.

313
Emperor Constantine
converts to Christianity,
which later becomes the
official religion of the
Roman Empire.

654
Start of the Arab
invasion. The coast east
of Silifke becomes Arab,
Islamic territory. The
troubled Byzantine
Empire has to fend off
Arabs, Persians,
Armenians and Bulgars
over the next 350 years.

1071
Selçuk Turks defeat the
Byzantine army. Over the
next 400 years, they
gradually conquer
Anatolia and impose their
name, language and
culture on the people,
creating Turkiye (the
place of the Turk) and the
Turkish nation.

1080–1375
Part of Cilicia breaks

Kemal Atatürk – father of modern Turkey

away from the Byzantine Empire to form the independent Christian state of Armenia.

1096
The Crusades begin as Western European armies confront the advance of Islam. The Fourth Crusade is in 1204.

1098–1268
Antioch becomes a Norman, Christian principality.

1288
A minor Muslim warlord, Osman Ghazi, begins to gain power in central Anatolia. The empire he began slowly grows over the next 150 years.

1453
Constantinople is captured; Emperor Constantine IX dies fighting on the walls and the city becomes Istanbul (Islamboul – the City of Islam). The Byzantine Empire is at an end; Turkey begins 450 years of Ottoman rule.

1909
The last Ottoman Sultan, Abdul Hamid, is deposed by the 'Young Turks'.

1914
Turkey enters World War I as a German ally; Mustafa Kemal leads victorious resistance at Gallipoli in the Dardanelles in 1915.

1919
Kemal leads the Turkish War of Independence and throws out all foreigners.

1923
Turkey is carved up in peace treaties. Kemal, now called Atatürk (Father of the Turks) becomes president of the new republic of Turkey. Greece and Turkey exchange minority populations. Atatürk begins reforming constitution (votes for women, equal rights, disestablishing religion and adopting the Latin alphabet), ruling as

a benevolent dictator. He dies in 1938.

1939–45
Turkey remains neutral during World War II.

1945
President İnönü turns Turkey into a parliamentary democracy.

1946
Turkey becomes a charter member of the United Nations.

1952
Turkey joins NATO.

1960–present
There are military coups in 1960, 1971 and 1980. Each time, the military stabilises the crisis then restores democracy. The biggest problems facing Turkey are the dispute with Greece over northern Cyprus, the Kurdish separatist movement, an unstable currency and economy, and relentless pressure towards Islamic fundamentalism.

11

Peace and Quiet

In spite of extensive development, there are still huge areas of the coast empty of everything but flowers. Of course, the easiest way to get some real peace and quiet is simply to travel out of season (between October and April), when you are quite likely to be the only guest at the hotel, the only tourist at the archaeological sight, and the only shivering soul on the beach.

Deserted Beaches

To f nd a deserted beach in the more popular areas requires some ingenuity and the climbing skills of a mountain goat, as they tend to be tiny coves tucked into the base of a cliff. If you are content to stay in a basic *pansiyon* (➤ 102), head east of Alanya, where the cliffs protect several small settlements with magnificent beaches as yet untouched by commerce. Beyond Mersin, the water is likely to be heavily polluted.

Sail Away

The best way to get away from it all on the water is to hire one of the traditional wooden *gülets* for the day or week, and sail off into a Mediterranean sunset. Most sleep between eight and twelve, in comfortable if tiny double cabins, with *en suite* shower and toilet, a communal indoor lounge and plenty of deck space, some shaded. They have the option of sail, although they more commonly use motors, and staff are on hand to do all housekeeping and

Flowers provide a blaze of colour throughout the spring and summer

The vivid colour of the copper-saturated sea gives the Turquoise Coast its name

catering. They will deliver you to sea caves and hidden coves inaccessible from land, to tiny, deserted islands and to sparkling bays, and if none of that inspires, you can simply dive over the side; most have swimming platforms and snorkelling equipment. Numerous tour operators both abroad and in Turkey will take bookings, and for shorter periods it is sometimes possible to deal direct with the captain. No children under 12 are allowed unless you charter the entire boat.

Green Lungs

All the major cities have parks that provide a cool, shady hideaway from the heat and noise, although the juice and postcard-sellers remain ever present (most are on the seafront). In Antalya, Karaoğlanoğlu Park is a wonderful 70,000sq m clifftop oasis, near Hadrian's Gate (➤ 54), with avenues of palms and excellent views. In Adana, a pleasant promenade stretches along the river from the Merkez Cami to the Taş Köprü (➤ 74).

A babbling river beloved of trout and whitewater canoeists flows through the Köprülü Kanyon

National Parks

A few miles inland, the jagged bulk of the Taurus Mountains creates a wild, spectacular barrier between the coast and the Anatolian plain.

Along them, several areas, many surrounding noteworthy archaeological sites, have been designated as National Parks. All offer excellent mountain hiking, together with the less energetic pleasures of flower-, butterfly- and bird-watching. The first spring flowers appear in February with an early carpet of mauve, pink and scarlet anemones. Within a month, the mountains are swathed in vivid yellow gorse and broom and by April and May the area is alive with oleander and orchids, jasmine and bougainvillea. The parks include Beydağlar Olympos Milli Parkı (➤ 44), Karatepe Milli Parkı (➤ 20), Köprülü Kanyon (➤ 64) and Güllükdaği Termessos Milli Parkı (➤ 48).

The Olympus National Park provides excellent opportunities for hiking and bird-watching

Southern Turkey's Famous

Divine Celebrities
Even the gods visited this coast. Leto brought her children, Apollo and Artemis, to the Letoön (➤ 42) to escape the jealous wrath of Zeus's wife, Hera. There was a famous oracle of Apollo at Patara, and it was supposedly in Daphne (Harbiye ➤ 83) that Paris gave the fateful golden apple to Aphrodite in return for the world's most beautiful woman, Helen – thereby sparking off the Trojan Wars.

St Paul

Paul (originally known as Saul) was born in about AD 10 in Tarsus, between Mersin and Adana on the south coast. He was a Jew, Roman citizen, tent-maker, rabbi and Pharisee, who eagerly persecuted the Christians until a blinding vision on the road to Damascus converted him to Christianity. He promptly channelled all his missionary zeal into spreading Christianity to the Gentiles, keeping in touch with his fledgling churches through copious letters that answered many fundamental questions of law, ethics and doctrine. These helped to form the basic rules of the church. In about AD 58, he was arrested and spent several years in prison before being executed in Rome.

St Nicholas (Father Christmas)

Born in Patara in about AD 300, Nicholas became bishop of Myra (➤ 32), and was imprisoned for his Christianity by

the Roman emperor Diocletian. When Constantine converted to Christianity Nicholas was released, and served as a delegate at the crucial first Council of Nicaea in AD 325. He is said to have left purses of gold as dowries for three girls who faced a life of prostitution; to have brought back to life three children who had been chopped up and pickled by a butcher, and to have performed numerous other miracles and acts of kindness. As patron saint of Greece, Russia, prisoners, sailors, travellers, unmarried girls and merchants, pawnbrokers and children, he has a huge cult following throughout Europe (his feast day is 6 December), and is widely associated with Santa Claus – derived from Sinterklaas, a Dutch variant of his name.

Famous Visitors

The great Egyptian pharaoh, Rameses II, sacked the Hittite city of Açana Höyük in 1285 BC; Alexander the Great romped through in 334 BC, and, in 65

St Paul of Tarsus did more than any man except Jesus to promote the spread of Christianity

BC, the Roman general Pompey rampaged along the coast. Julius Caesar was the first of many Roman emperors to visit (in 47 BC) and in 41 BC, Mark Anthony met Cleopatra here. Of many early Christian visitors, the most important was St Peter, who lived in Antakya between AD 47 and 54.

Top Ten

Above: *the Roman theatre, Aspendos*

Right: *Turkey's cities were also art galleries*

1
Alanya: İç Kale

📍 28C2

✉️ Castle Road, central Alanya

🕐 Daily 8–7

🍴 Soft drinks stands

🚢 From the harbour below (▶ 60)

♿ None

✋ Moderate

↔️ Alanya city (▶ 57–60)

Surrounded on three sides by sheer sea cliffs, there has been a fort crowning Alanya's towering castle rock for at least 2,500 years.

A massive 250m rock promontory slices flat, sprawling Alanya in two, its top encircled by the huge defensive walls of the İç Kale (Inner Citadel). From its battlements, you get an idea of the citadel's true size. The outer curtain reaches right back to the harbour, surrounding the whole steeply stacked old town with a 7km wall, complete with 150 bastions, including the Kızıl Kule (Red Tower, ▶ 59) and around 400 water cisterns. It took 12 years to build.

Although the town's earliest incarnation was as the Hellenistic frontier post of Coracesium, the first known fort was built in the 2nd century BC by a pirate, Diodotos Tryphon, and destroyed by Pompey in 67 BC. Mark Anthony later gave the town to Cleopatra. In 1221, it fell to the Selçuk Sultan Alâeddin Keykubad I, who rebuilt the fort as the formidable construction visible today.

Few structures that are within the citadel remain intact,

The vast citadel at Alanya was the crowning achievement of Selçuk Sultan Alâeddin Keykubad I

although there is a small Byzantine church with some fading frescoes. The real attraction is the dizzying view from its walls. A fenced platform marks the Hurling Rock, or local execution point. Legend says that the condemned man was given a pebble to throw: if it landed in the water, he was freed; if it hit rock, he was heaved over the edge.

There are nearly 5km of steep hairpin bends up to the walls of the İç Kale (allow an hour) – a taxi is worth every lira; the more energetic may find the walk down through the partially ruinous old town rewarding (▶ 58).

2
Antalya Müzesi

This museum holds a world-class collection of classical sculpture, prehistoric and ethnographic exhibits from Mediterranean Turkey.

 28B2

 Kenan Evren Bulvarı, Konyaaltı; 2km west of the town centre

0242 241 4528

Tue–Sun 8:30–5. Closed Mon

Café with drinks and light snacks (£)

Dolmuş (shared taxi) or taxi

Few, access reasonable

Moderate

Museum shop in the main foyer, Dösem Ministry of Culture shop in the grounds

Above: *an elaborately carved sarcophagus*

Below: *a statue from the museum*

The number of exhibits on display in Antalya's spacious, purpose-built archaeological museum is not huge, but immense care has gone into presentation, lighting and explanation. Each piece is seen at its best and can be appreciated not only for its artistry, but for its place in the long, long history of Mediterranean Turkey.

The tour begins with a children's room containing a charmingly detailed model village and tables where children can play under supervision, while their parents wander round. A small natural history section then gives way to detailed prehistoric record, with tools such as palaeolithic scrapers, awls, hand axes and arrowheads from the Karain Mağarası (➤ 37), Bronze Age burials, jewellery and toys from the Elmalı area (➤ 41) and early pottery from Aspendos (➤ 18).

Magnificent 2nd-century statues from Perge (➤ 24) introduce the classical era and the Graeco-Roman pantheon in the Gallery of the Gods. Beyond are other Roman and Byzantine statues, sarcophagi, figurines and a fascinating display of amphorae and other goods recovered from early shipwrecks.

Next come collections of coins, mosaics, 19th- and 20th-century icons, and the supposed reliquary of St Nicholas (➤ 14). The final few rooms deal with later Turkish lifestyle and civilisation. Wide-ranging displays cover everything from the *hamam* (Turkish bath) to carpets, traditional dress, ceramic tiles, musical instruments and several reconstructed rooms.

Outside, pleasant, shady gardens are filled with yet more urns, sarcophagi and statues.

3
Aspendos

This sweeping hemisphere of seats gives Aspendos fine acoustics

For the last 2,000 years, the world's greatest performers – from gladiators to Pavarotti – have graced the theatre of this ancient Pamphylian city.

✚ 28C2

✉ 49km east of Antalya, 5km off the N-400 through the village of Belkis

🕐 Theatre daily May–Sep 8–7; Oct–Apr 8–5:30

🍴 Drinks stands outside; restaurants on the approach road (££)

🚌 *Dolmuş*

♿ None, partial access

✋ Moderate

↔ Antalya (► 17 and 53–6), Perge (► 24–5), Kurşunlu Şelâlesi (► 67), Side (► 68), Sillyon (► 69)

❓ Dösem Ministry of Culture shop in the entrance; souvenir stands outside; shops on the approach road. Festivals of folk music and dance, opera, ballet and film held in the theatre (► 116)

Aspendos proudly boasts what is probably the world's finest surviving Roman theatre. It was designed by an architect named Xeno, son of Theodoro, during the reign of Emperor Marcus Aurelius (AD 161–80) and donated to the city by two brothers, Curtius Crispinus and Curtius Auspicatus. The huge, semi-circular auditorium has seating for 15,000, with 40 rows of marble seats divided by 10 staircases in the lower section and 21 above. At the top is a vaulted gallery. The massive acoustic stage wall was originally richly decorated, faced in marble with 40 free-standing columns and niches for statues, many of which are now in Antalya's Archaeological Museum (► 17). It would have had a wooden sound board at the top and a wooden stage about 1.5m above ground level, projecting out 7m. Doors below the stage were used to release animals during wild beast shows. There are also some additions, made in the 13th century, when the theatre was used as a Selçuk caravansaray.

Aspendos was a prosperous city, probably founded in the 12th century BC, and specialising in luxury goods such as gold- and silver-embroidered *kilims* (carpets), lemon-wood furniture, wine and horses. The theatre rightly grabs the glory, but there are many other remains. On the left, as you approach the theatre, are a 3rd-century AD bath house and gymnasium. On the hill behind it stand a Roman agora (market place), a fountain, a Byzantine basilica and an 880m section of aqueduct. Directly north of the theatre are the Roman stadium and Hellenistic necropolis. To the right, an elegant 13th-century Selçuk stone bridge crosses the Köprüçay (ancient Eurymedon River).

4
Hatay Müzesi
(Antakya Museum)

Antakya's museum is a rainbow of magnificent mosaics, most rescued from Roman villas at nearby Daphne (Harbiye).

🕂 29F1

✉ Gündüz Caddesi 1, Antakya

☎ 0326-214 6167

🕐 Tue–Sun 8:30–12, 1:30–5. Closed Mon

🍴 Café in summer only; old town restaurants within easy walking distance (££)

🚌 *Dolmuş*

♿ None, but access good

✋ Moderate

↔ Antakya (➤ 80–2), Harbiye (➤ 83), Çevlik (➤ 83), St Simeon's Monastery (➤ 90)

The museum begins with a small collection of costumes and jewellery, but this is merely an overture. Round the corner are four galleries containing a breathtaking array of some 50 huge, beautifully preserved mosaics. Together they make up one of the finest collections of mosaics in the world – enough to make the long, cross-country journey to Antakya worthwhile.

The earliest known mosaics date back to 4th-millennium BC Mesopotamia, but the technique only really became widespread in the 1st century AD. Most of those on show here belong to the 2nd–4th centuries AD, when they were used to decorate floors and, less commonly, walls. By this stage, the minute chips of marble and granite had been joined by semi-precious stones, glass and glazed ceramics to create a quite extraordinarily subtle range of colours. Some of the mosaics are intricate abstract patterns; most depict classical legends, the gods, the seasons, the surrounding wildlife and feasts, with a realism and depth worthy of a painting. In particular, look out for *The Four Seasons* (Gallery 1); *The Buffet Mosaic* (Gallery 2); *The Negro Fisherman* and a constipated baby Hercules in *Hercules Strangling Serpents* (Gallery 3).

The space between them is used for sculptures. Gallery 5 holds various Assyrian and Hittite statues and inscriptions, and the last two rooms contain a broad collection of coins, pottery, glass, jewellery and other small artefacts. These, in turn, lead to an open colonnade and small garden with a few more mosaics, several sculptures, sarcophagi and inscribed stelae.

Roman residences at Daphne were decorated with superb mosaics, now in Antakya Museum

5
Karatepe

29F2

110km northeast of Adana; turn off the N-400 after 80km at Osmaniye; the next 20km are on potholed tar, the final 10km on gravel

Daily May–Sep, 8:30–12:30, 2–5:30; Oct–Apr 8–12, 1–3:30. Guided tours only

Snack stand outside the gate (£); picnic area on the hill overlooking the lake outside the sight

None

Cheap (car park fee)

Misis (➤ 85), Topprakale (➤ 91), Yılankalesi (➤ 92)

Strictly no photography

A last surviving remnant of the powerful Hittite civilisation, Karatepe's story-board carvings still guard the entrances to a long-vanished citadel.

Known to the Hittites as Aslantaş ('Aslan's place'), Karatepe stands on a rock outcrop surrounded on three sides by the huge Çeyhan reservoir. The wooded site alone is wonderful, but the few Hittite remains, carefully preserved *in situ* in an open-air museum, are something very special indeed.

The formidably walled frontier castle and summer palace was built during the final throes of the Hittite Empire, in the 8th century BC, by a local ruler named Azatiwata. It was abandoned after being sacked and burned by Assyrian invaders in the mid-7th century BC.

The tour follows a 1km-long circular path along part of the heavily rebuilt castle walls and through the woods to visit the two main gates, both flamboyantly decorated with sculptures. The inner walls are lined with reliefs and large tracts of very entertaining Hittite hieroglyphics with almost cartoon-like drawings. The reality, of course, is far more serious: the first inscription in the upper group boastfully records the building of the city, and the peace and prosperity of the region, and threatens with the wrath of the gods anyone who dares disturb the gate. (Ironically, the gate survived but the castle and kingdom did not.) Much of it is thoughtfully also written in Phoenician, providing archaeologists with the key to deciphering the language.

The relief sculptures cover a wide range of subjects, including gods, happy feasts, vicious battle scenes, bear-baiting, a tender portrait of a woman suckling her child, splendidly snarling lions and sphinx gates. The second (lower) group has been more heavily restored, but both are in good condition.

Hittite relief sculptures provide a vivid record of daily life and great events 1200 years BC

6
Kaş

One of the most upmarket resorts along the coast, Kaş has been protected from over-development by its lack of beaches.

Many Greek cottages in Kaş have been converted to shops or restaurants

Until 1923, the Greek community of Andifli made its living exporting timber. Then came the mass exchange of population (Kaya, ➤ 38); the Greeks left, and the renamed Kaş (meaning 'eyebrow', after the curved bay) sank back into being a fishing village – until the 1980s tourism boom.

These days, there are few large hotels; the nearest sand beach, at Kaputaş, 14km west, is only 150m long and at the bottom of a steep cliff; and with the Taurus mountains plunging straight into the sea, there is little available development land. Yet Kaş is undoubtedly the most sophisticated resort along the Mediterranean coast (after Antalya): a remarkably pretty town, with excellent restaurants (➤ 95), delightful small hotels, unparalleled nightlife, and superb shopping, specialising in high-quality (and price) designer jewellery, clothes and magnificent hand-made carpets (➤ 106–9).

There is even a little history. The town is built over ancient Antiphellos, the port for Phellos (➤ 45). There is a small Hellenistic theatre about 500m from the town centre on Hastane Caddesi (towards the peninsula), a Doric tomb with a frieze of dancing girls on the hill 100m beyond, and a free-standing Lycian 'lion tomb' on Postane Sokak. The 500m cliff behind is dotted with house tombs.

There are fabulous views of the town and the surrounding bay from the end of the peninsula and from the eastern mountain-top approach along the N-400 from Finike. Boat tours call at Kekova (➤ 38) and a tiny island with a Crusader castle, Kastellórizo (Meis in Turkish), 3km off-shore and still owned by Greece.

➕ 28B1

✉ 107km southeast of Fethiye; 181km southwest of Antalya, on the N-400

🍽 Choice of restaurants (£–££)

🚌 *Dolmuş*; bus from Antalya and Fethiye

⛴ From the harbour and local travel agents

ℹ Cumhuriyet Meydanı 5 ☎ 0242-836 1230

♿ None

🔁 Demre (➤ 31–2), Kalkan (➤ 37), Kekova (➤ 38), Letoön (➤ 42), Phellos (➤ 45), Pınara (➤ 46), Saklıkent and Sidyma (➤ 47), Tlos, Xanthos (➤ 49)

7
Mamure Kalesi (Anamur Castle)

✚ 29D1

✉ 5km east of Anamur town on the N-400

🕐 Daily 8:30–5:30

🍴 Several small restaurants (£)

🚌 *Dolmuş* from Anamur to entrance

♿ None

✋ Cheap; a local guide is worthwhile

↔ Anamur (► 78)

Romantically sited staring out to sea, with the waves crashing around the walls, this is a castle to gladden the heart of any medieval knight.

Mamure Kalesi is probably the finest of the many castles dotting the Cilician landscape. There has been a fortress here since the 3rd century AD, and by the 10th century, the first version of the present castle was in place, a formidable stronghold of notorious pirates. From the late 11th century, it was owned by the Kings of Armenia, but in 1226 the coast was conquered by the great Selçuk builder, Sultan Alâeddin Keykubad I, who virtually razed it and rebuilt it from the ground upwards. Between 1300 and 1308, Karamanoğlu ruler Mahmut Bey took control. The following century, it became a last foothold on the mainland for the crusading Lusignan kings of Cyprus, who had absorbed the title, if not the lands, of the King of Armenia. Finally, in the late 15th century, it fell into Ottoman hands and remained in use right through World War I.

Today, once again restored and open to the public, it is a powerful and imposing place, with massive curtain walls sheltering two enormous courtyards. There is a small, heavily restored mosque in the centre, but the real treat is to explore the dark living rooms built into the thickness of the walls (take a torch), and to scramble along the windy battlements between the 36 bastions.

Anamur stands on the southernmost point of ancient Anatolia. It is said that on a clear day from the walls you can see Cyprus, some 70km off-shore. Even on hazier days, the view along the seaward wall to the waves pounding on the rocks beneath is magnificent.

Mamure Kalesi, its feet washed by the waves, is one of Europe's most romantic castles

8
Patara

Once the most important port on the Lycian coast, Patara is now a scattering of overgrown ruins behind an 18km-long beach of white sand.

Patara's white-gold sands have been voted amongst the world's best beaches

According to legend, Apollo spent his winters in Patara, which was home to a famous oracle (said to rival that in Delphi), also an important trading centre, and one of the most powerful cities of the Lycian federation. In 42 BC, Brutus and Cassius arrived, looking for loot to fund their war against Mark Anthony and Octavian. They took the women hostage but released them unharmed when the men refused to submit, showing themselves to be civilised. The grateful men paid up. St Nicholas was born here in the 4th century AD (► 14). The city eventually died in the Middle Ages, when the harbour silted up and became a reedy swamp.

The site, scattered through fields across a large plain, is almost entirely unexcavated. Highlights amongst the many ruins include a triumphal arch, built in AD 100 by the governor, Mettius Modestus, and used as part of an aqueduct; a theatre, now filled with sand; two bath complexes; a temple to Athena; a huge granary built by Hadrian; a lighthouse, and numerous tombs. The temple and oracle of Apollo have not yet been discovered.

A boardwalk beyond the ancient city leads to the magnificent beach, with excellent swimming, surfing and windsurfing. With so much space, there is always an uncrowded patch. There is no natural shade, and there are relatively few drinks stands, so go prepared.

In season (May–October) this is a breeding ground for turtles. Because of this and its historic importance, much of the coast is protected, but hotels are springing up on the unprotected extremities and in the village of Gelemiş, 3km inland.

✝ 28A1

✉ Turn off the N-400 9km west of Kalkan; the site is 8km from the turn-off, the beach access about 1km beyond the site

🕐 Archaeological site and beach both open daily, May–Sep 7:30–7; Oct–Apr 8:30–5; on foot both are open access (the barrier is about 2km from the beach)

🍴 Numerous options in Gelemiş (£)

🚌 Bus to Gelemiş

🚐 From Kaş and Kalkan and from the village to the site and beach

♿ None

✋ Cheap, plus car park charge at the beach

↔ Kaş (► 21), Kalkan (► 37), Kekova (► 38), Letoön (► 42), Phellos (► 45), Pınara (► 46), Saklıkent and Sidyma (► 47), Tlos, Xanthos (► 49)

23

9
Perge

🕂 28B2

✉ 15km due east of Antalya, off the N-400. Turn off the main road at Aksu; the ruins are 2km from the turning

🌐 Daily May–Sep 7:30–7; Oct–Apr 8–5:30

🍴 Café and souvenir shop near the ticket booth (£)

🚌 *Dolmuş* or taxi from Antalya to the entrance

♿ None

🖐 Moderate, plus parking fee

↔ Aspendos (► 18), Antalya (► 53–6), Kurşunlu Falls (► 67), Köprülü Kanyon (► 64), Side (► 68)

Perge is the best excavated, most complete and easily accessible of the ancient cities along the south coast of Turkey.

Although it was known to the Hittites in about 1300 BC as Parha, little else is known about Perge until 333 BC, when the city welcomed Alexander the Great, who used it as his base throughout the Pamphylian campaign. Following his death, control passed first to the Seleucids, then to Pergamum (on the Aegean coast), and in 133 BC to Rome, under whose wing the city flourished. However, during the Byzantine era the river silted up, leaving the busy trading port stranded 12km from the sea, and Perge slowly declined. Excavation and restoration began in 1947, and many magnificent sculptures found here are now in the Antalya Archaeological Museum (Antalya Müzesi ► 17).

Before reaching the main site, the access road passes a 14,000-seat theatre on the left and, to the right, a huge stadium with seating for 12,000, both built in the 2nd century AD.

Visitors enter the main site through a triumphal Roman

Above: *elaborately carved column bases give a small idea of the glory that was ancient Perge*

gate. To the left are a nymphaeum (ornamental fountain) dedicated to the city's deity, Artemis Pergaea, and the Southern Bath House, the largest and grandest in the city, both built in the reign of Septimius Severus (AD 193–211).

Directly in front are the two massive red-stone towers of the 3rd-century BC Hellenistic Gate. Between them is a horseshoe-shaped courtyard, lovingly decorated by Plancia Magna, daughter of the governor, between AD 120 and 122, but now permanently flooded; much of her finely carved marble lies in heaps. Bear right, along the main path, to reach the 4th-century AD agora (market place), surrounded by a colonnade with a mosaic floor and shops. The small circular temple in the centre was possibly dedicated to Hermes, the patron of merchants. From here Main Street, a 300m-long, marble-paved avenue, lined with columns and stepped pavements, leads through the city. A 2m-wide water channel runs down the centre and chariot marks are still visible. About halfway along, a second main road crosses, dividing the city into four quarters. Buildings along the way include a Byzantine basilica, a 1st-century AD palaestra (gymnasium) and, at the far end, another elaborate fountain. Beyond this, a path snakes up the 60m acropolis to the site of the earliest city, of which little remains.

Inset: the Hellenistic Gate marks the official entrance to the Greek city of Perge

Bottom: Perge's colonnaded agora would once have been alive with shops and market stalls

10
Phaselis

28B2

✉ 18km south of Kemer, 3km off the N-400; the site is 1km beyond the ticket booth

🕐 Daily May–Oct 7:30–7; Nov–Apr 8–5:30

🍴 Simple café (£) near the ticket booth, drinks stand in the car park; numerous restaurants in nearby Tekirova (£–£££)

🚌 *Dolmuş* to turning off main road (3km)

♿ None

✋ Moderate, plus car charge

↔ Olympos and the Chimaera (➤ 44)

Once ships filled the three small harbours of wealthy Phaselis; today, it is in atmospheric ruins, its shady bays excellent for swimming.

Phaselis is one of the prettiest, most easily accessible and most peaceful of all the ancient cities along the coast. It is an ideal place to take a towel, a picnic and a good book and spend the day sightseeing, sunbathing and swimming off one of its idyllic little sandy beaches, fringed with pines.

Legend claims Phaselis was founded by 7th-century BC colonists from Rhodes, who paid for the land with dried fish. They were ousted by the Persians, who ruled for 130 years until the arrival of the Lycians. Alexander the Great was welcomed with open arms in 334 BC, and used Phaselis as his winter base. The city prospered as a trading port, exporting timber, rose oil and perfumes, until the 13th century AD, when it was eventually abandoned. Its citizens enjoyed a poor reputation, however: the Greek orator Demosthenes (c383–22 BC) went so far as to call them 'the most scoundrelly and unscrupulous of men'.

Most of the surviving ruins belong to the Roman and

Sunset and a fleet of gülets add even more romance to the ancient harbour at Phaselis

Byzantine periods. There are three small harbours: the heavily fortified north harbour was rarely used because of its exposed position; the central harbour took military and small trading vessels, while the south harbour was used by larger trading ships. The main street, lined with columns, shops, several agorae and bath houses, crosses the headland between them. At one end is an imposing gate, erected for the state visit of Emperor Hadrian in AD 131. On the hill above is a small, unrestored theatre, and inland are an imposing aqueduct, a necropolis and some early Hellenistic structures.

What to See

Above: *the beautiful deep blue waters of the lagoon at Ölüdeniz*

Right: *the crescent moon and star of the Turkish flag*

TURKEY SOUTH COAST

Konya

Karaman

Göksu

715

Alahan

Ermenek

Mut

os Dağları

Cilicia

Niğde

3480m

E90/0-21

750

Karatepe

Anavarza

Ceyhan

E90/0-52

Bahçe

Yılankalesi

Osmaniye

Toprakkale

625

Pompeiopolis

Uzuncaburç

Cennet ve Cehennem Deresi

Korykos ve Kız Kalesi

Narlıkuyu

Mersin

Tarsus

Adana

İncirlik

Misis

Seyhan

Tuzla

E91/0-53

Dörtyol

Yumurtalık

İskenderun Körfezi

İskenderun

Silifke

Gülnar

Taşucu

Karataş

Kırıkhan

Mamure Kalesi

400

Reyhanlı

Anamur

Aydıncık

Ovacık

Antakya

Anamorium

Çevlik

Samandağ

Harbiye

E97/825

SYR

0   100   200 km

D   E   F

Lycia

The most important maritime kingdom on the coast of ancient Anatolia first came to prominence in the 8th century BC, although there are mentions of the Lycian people (then known as the Lukka) 500 years earlier. They were thriving merchants and sailors, originally from Crete, whose cities were organised by King Pericles in the 4th century BC into the Lycian League. Today all that is left of the Lycians is their immense and elaborate rock tombs, carved into the cliff faces and mountain tops.

This is the most scenically beautiful region of Turkey's Mediterranean coast, with the wild, towering Taurus mountains plunging straight to the sea, forming a coastline of jagged rocks and mysterious sea caves. Until 1981, the area was isolated and ignored. All that is changing fast, but the lack of long sandy beaches has helped slow the rate of development.

> *'This maritime tract is rugged, and difficult to be approached, but has very good harbours, and is inhabited by a people who are not inclined to violence.'*
>
> STRABO,
> *The Geography*
> (c54 BC–AD 24)

Previous page: tourists admire the rock tombs at Kaunos

Left: *Myra's spectacular rock tombs*

Demre (Kale)

Set on a broad-bottomed alluvial plain, with hothouses on every available inch of land, this rather scruffy town, officially called Kale, is known by absolutely everyone as Demre. The modern town has little to offer, but the ancient sites are fascinating (➤ 32).

Just to the south of Demre is the little seaside village of Çayağzi, built on the ancient harbour of Andriake. The village has a very pleasant harbour front, with several fish restaurants and a landscaped walkway, a small beach, thriving boat yards, and a massive Roman granary: this was built by Hadrian between AD 119 and 139 and used as a central supply depot for the entire empire. In season, there are *gület* trips to Kekova.

What to See in Demre

MYRA ✪✪
Myra was one of the earliest and most important of the cities in the Lycian federation, dating back to the 5th century BC. Today, the ruins stand under the cliff behind Demre, with a complete free-standing theatre which was converted in the 2nd century AD for gladiatorial combat. Look for the fallen frieze of theatrical masks in the remains of the stage building. Behind the theatre, tiers of magnificent Lycian house tombs rise up the cliff. The agora, probably east of the theatre, is still unexcavated, but there are remains of a 5th-century BC fortress on the acropolis above and a further group of tombs to the northeast of the main site, including the so-called Painted Tomb. The paint has faded, but the relief carvings of a family feast are still remarkable.

➕ 28B1
🖂 46km east of Kaş, 27km west of Finike; Andriake 3km south of Demre
🚌 *Dolmuş*
♿ None
🔄 Finike (➤ 36), Kekova (➤ 38)
❓ Camel-wrestling contests in Jan/Feb (➤ 116)

➕ 28B1
🖂 1km north of Demre
🕐 Daily May–Sep 7:30–7; Oct–Apr 8–5:30
🚌 *Dolmuş* to Demre town centre
♿ None
🖐 Cheap
🔄 Finike (➤ 36), Kekova (➤ 38)

Right: *remote Arykanda has one of the finest settings of any city*
Below: *tombs record the lives of their inhabitants*

➕ 28B1
✉ Demre centre: clearly signed
🕐 Daily 8:30–4:30
🚌 *Dolmuş*
♿ None
✋ Moderate
↔ Finike (➤ 36), Kekova (➤ 38)
❓ Badly flooded in Feb 1998, may still be undergoing restoration. Feast of St Nicholas, 6 December.

NOEL BABA KİLESİ

St Nicholas (➤ 14) was bishop of Myra in the 4th century AD, his miracles adding to the city's fame. The first church on this site probably dated from his time; a basilica was built over his tomb in the 6th century, but was destroyed almost immediately by Arab raiders. Repaired by the Emperor Justinian, it was again restored and extended by Constantine IX in 1043, and by the Russians in the 19th century. In 1087, Nicholas's body was stolen by Italian traders and taken to the 11th-century basilica of San Nicola in Bari, Italy.

Today, there are some early segments in the charming little church, now 5m below street level and dwarfed by the 19th-century bell tower, upper storey and monastery, and a hideous steel and plastic roof.

What to See in Lycia

ANDRİAKE (DEMRE, ➤ 31–2)

ARYKANDA (ARİF)

This is one of the most isolated, complete and spectacularly beautiful ancient cities in Lycia. Built vertically up the end of a deep valley, it remains a cool, green haven all year round, but in spring it is particularly decorative, with carpets of flowers, snow-capped mountain peaks and several small waterfalls.

➕ 28B2
✉ 35km north of Finike, off the Elmalı road (➤ 40–1 for access details)

Arykanda was probably founded in the 2nd millennium BC, but the first archaeological evidence dates to the 5th century BC. As with other Lycian cities, it was ruled successively by the Persians, Alexander, the Seleucids and the Ptolemies, joined the Lycian federation and became Roman in AD 43. After earthquakes in the 2nd, 3rd and 5th centuries AD, and Arab invasions in the 7th–8th centuries, the locals finally gave up and moved down the valley.

From the car park, the lower acropolis (to the right) includes the ruins of shops and a small 4th-century AD bath house. The tin-roofed sheds to the left protect the mosaic floors of a large Byzantine basilica. Further up the hill is the entertainment district, with an odeon (for musical performances), theatre, stadium, and the agora. The main path leads round to a magnificent bath complex, whose 10m-high arched ceilings, picture windows and mosaic floors are nearly intact. Near the cliff face are a gymnasium, an arcaded market, various paved streets and a Roman temple, later adapted for Christian worship. The necropolis is at the far eastern end of the site.

Open access
Small restaurant on the main road near the turning (£)
None
Cheap
Tour (➤ 40–1)

Did you know ?

In 1838–9, a British archaeologist, Sir Charles Fellows, led an expedition to Lycia. He rediscovered the remains of 13 ancient cities, including Tlos and Xanthos (➤ 49). He then stripped them of their finest friezes, sculptures and mosaics, shipping them all back to London. Most of his finds are on display in the British Museum.

Above: history the easy way – tourist boats cruise past the Dalyan tombs

 28A2

 97km west of Fethiye, 25km off the N-400 at Ortaca

All sights open access

Dolmuş; access to Kaunos by boat or foot only

None

All sights cheap

DALYAN AND KAUNOS ★★

The busy little tourist resort of Dalyan is inland, on the east bank of the broad Dalyan Çayı. There are no sights in the town itself, but it does have several good fish restaurants, serving ultra-fresh mullet and sea bass by the river. Boats provide transport to the beach and impressive rock tombs on the west bank.

To the north, the road winds for 13km along a huge freshwater lake, Köyceğiz Göyü. The surrounding swampy reed-beds are alive with birds, dragonflies, butterflies and other wildlife, while complicated barriers across the water catch grey mullet and sea bass as they return downstream after breeding. Also upstream, İlıca's smelly thermal mud baths are said to increase male potency and cure gynaecological problems and rheumatism – and they're fun.

On the coast, İztuzu Beach is a spectacular, 5km stretch of sand, with a healthy breeding colony of loggerhead turtles. Tourists are welcome during the day, but strict environmental regulations in breeding season (April–October) include a ban on beach umbrellas in case the poles damage the nests, so shade can be a little scarce.

Kaunos, 10km west, is a Hellenistic city, famous in its day for exporting salt and slaves, with 4th-century BC walls and a fort, a 2nd-century BC theatre, a huge Roman bath, currently under restoration, a Byzantine basilica and a variety of tombs, built by the local Carian people in the Lycian style.

The ruins are now 5km inland, the harbour having silted up over the centuries, leaving beautiful reed-beds swarming with terrapins, frogs and flamingoes. Boats dock 10 minutes' walk from the site.

Happy tourists wallowing in Dalyan mud baths

Turkish Delight comes in many flavours

FETHİYE 😊😊

This busy port and market town, tucked into a broad bay at the foot of Mount Crasus, marks both the western border of Lycia and the western end of the Taurus Mountains. The town has been here for at least 3,000 years, but has suffered periodic identity crises. Known to the Lycians as Telmessos and to the Byzantines as Anastasiopolis, it became Makri in 1424 under the Ottomans, finally changing its name again in 1934 in memory of a local pilot who died during the War of Independence, Fethi Bey. It suffered severe earthquakes in 1856 and 1957, leaving only a few fragmentary historical remains in a largely modern town.

Although its off-shoot beach resorts of Çalış (4km west of town) and Ölüdeniz are crammed throughout the season, Fethiye still remains, at least in part, a working Turkish town. Next to the yachts and tourist *gülets* in the marina are small, brightly painted fishing boats and giant freighters, loading chrome and vegetables from the docks where Lycians once loaded frankincense and myrrh.

There are several particularly grand Lycian tombs – in front of the Town Hall near the modern harbour, in the old town and, most magnificent of all, the 4th-century BC **Tomb of Amyntas**, carved into the sheer cliff behind the town. Just behind the tourist office, the amphitheatre has recently been excavated and is undergoing restoration. On top of the mountain is a ruined fort, thought to have been built in the 14th century by the Crusader Knights of St John, who were based on nearby Rhodes. Fragmentary Lycian, Greek and Byzantine remains are also visible. The town's small museum has archaeological remains from the region.

Parks and open-air cafés line the seafront, and there are plenty of bars, restaurants and other entertainments.

🔺 28A2
✉ 50km east of Dalaman airport; 225km west of Antalya
ℹ İskele Karşasi 1, opposite the main harbour
   ☎ 0252-614 1527
🚌 *Dolmuş*
🚢 Boat trips to various local islands; ferries to Rhodes (Greece)
♿ None; access to harbour area
↔ Ölüdeniz (➤ 43), Pınara (➤ 46), Saklıkent (➤ 47), Tlos (➤ 49)

Tomb of Amyntas
✉ Up the steps from Kaya Caddesi, behind the bus station
🕐 Daily 8:30–sunset
💰 Cheap

Museum
✉ Off Atatürk Caddesi
🕐 Tue–Sun 8:30–5. Closed Mon
💰 Moderate

<table>
</table>

☩ X28B1

✉ 140km southwest of
Antalya; 60km southwest
of Kemer; 77km east of
Kaş (**➤** 40–1 for details
of directions to Limyra)

◷ Open access

❙❙ Some restaurants (£–££)

🚌 Dolmuş to Finike and
Turunçova (3km from
Limyra)

♿ None

🖐 Free

Above: *every available
inch of land is crowded
with orchards and
greenhouses*

Opposite: *an attractive
setting and charming
cottages give Kalkan its
appeal*

FİNİKE AND LİMYRA ✪

Finike was a small fishing and agricultural village until the
main road sliced the town in half. Today, although there
are a couple of good restaurants overlooking the working
harbour and sweeping bay, and several small *pansiyons* on
the southern edge of town, tourism development has
remained relatively low-key. This is an attractive place for a
cheap, quiet holiday immersed in Turkish culture. There
are several fine old Ottoman buildings in the narrow
streets at the back of town, and the surrounding area is
renowned for its fruit, producing luscious honeydew
melons in summer, sweet winter oranges, and huge,
flavour-packed tomatoes all year round.

Limyra, 8km north, was the capital of King Pericles
(founder of the Lycian federation) in the 4th century BC. It
later became a Byzantine bishopric, but was abandoned
after heavy damage during 7th- to 9th-century Arab raids.
Many of the buildings are scattered through the modern
village, often doubling as garden walls. The almost square
buildings near the river were part of a Byzantine convent;
to the left is an imposing 2nd-century AD theatre. Above all,
this is the site of the largest necropolis in Lycia: the stony
hillside is peppered with tombs, from the simple to the
grandiose. One of the most elaborate is the free-standing
4th-century BC tomb of Catabara, just beyond the theatre,
its reliefs depicting a funeral banquet and the judgement of
the dead. Right at the top, involving a severe 40-minute
scramble, is the Heroön, the tomb of Pericles himself, its
frieze showing scenes from the life of the hero.

KALKAN ✪✪✪

Without a doubt the prettiest of the small resorts along the Lycian coast, Kalkan is a latecomer to tourism. It was once a Greek village that made a poor living from fishing, charcoal-burning and olives. The rich moved inland to Bezırgan, leaving the Ottoman houses untouched, to be redeveloped as delightful shops, restaurants and *pansiyons*. Built down the side of a deep valley, its narrow, bougainvillea-draped streets tumbling into a tiny harbour (now a smart marina), Kalkan is a very upmarket place with excellent food and shopping and easy access to numerous historic sights. The only local beaches are man-made; the nearest natural sand beaches are tiny Kaputaş (6km east), shared with Kaş, and vast Patara (19km west).

28A1

⊠ 26km west of Kaş, on the N-400

🍴 Wide choice (£-££)

🚌 *Dolmuş*

🚫 None

💠 Kaş (➤ 21), Patara (➤ 23), Kekova (➤ 38), Demre (➤ 31), Letoön (➤ 42), Phellos (➤ 45), Pınara (➤ 46), Saklıkent and Sidyma (➤ 47), Tlos, Xanthos (➤ 49)

KARAİN MAĞARASI (KARAIN CAVE) ✪✪

Rediscovered by Guiseppe Moretti (➤ 64) in 1919, Karain was an ideal home: a healthy, south-facing cave 370m above sea level and a safe 80m above the plain, with a good water supply and a rich local food supply. The first humans moved in about 30,000 years ago, and it remained inhabited for some 20,000 years. The cave has proved to be the single most important prehistoric site in Turkey, producing an almost continuous stream of fascinating finds, from hippopotamus bones to hand axes and arrowheads, and the skull of a Neanderthal child. There are three large caverns: the first two were used for living, the third as a place of refuge, a cemetery and, during the classical period, as a temple. All three have stalactites and stalagmites. There are stairs, proper lighting and a small but detailed site museum.

28B2

⊠ 27km northwest of Antalya, off the N-650 to Burdur; the cave is about 6km from the main road

🕐 Daily 8:30–5

🚫 None

💷 Cheap

💠 Termessos (➤ 48)

❓ Many finds are in the Museum of Anatolian Civilisations in Ankara and the Antalya Archaeological Museum (➤ 17)

KAŞ (➤ 21, TOP TEN)

🚩 28A2
✉ 7km south of Fethiye
🕐 Open access
♿ None
🎟 Free
↔ Ölüdeniz (➤ 43)

KAYAKÖY ✪

Kaya, on the site of ancient Karmylassos, is the modern equivalent of all those abandoned ancient cities. Until 1923, it was a thriving village of around 3,500 people, most of them Greek Orthodox, who had settled here from the Dodecanese. After Atatürk won Turkey's independence, he threw all the foreigners out, and they were deported along with nearly a million others. The Macedonian Muslims who were shipped into Turkey in the massive exchange of population believed Kaya to be cursed, and it was abandoned. It is now an eerily complete ghost village with over 1,500 homes, of which only a handful, on the fringes, have been redeveloped for tourism, due to legal wranglings over ownership.

🚩 28B1
✉ 30km east of Kaş by road; turn off the N-400 after 11km and follow signs to Üçağız
🚢 In season, there are regular full-day *gület* trips to Kekova from Kaş, Kalkan and Andriake.
🍴 Several excellent fish restaurants in Kaleüçağız and Simena (£–££)
🎟 Simena castle cheap; boat trip expensive
↔ Kaş (➤ 21)

KEKOVA ADASI ✪✪

The long, skinny island of Kekova is reached by boat – one of the most popular excursions on the Lycian coast, usually including several other sights.

Start from the tiny harbour in Üçağız, a pretty little village, with a few shops, restaurants and simple *pansiyons*, now protected from further development. On the rocks to the east, all that remains of the ancient city of Teimiussa is a Lycian necropolis, with some partly submerged tombs.

Around the headland, Kale is accessible only by water. Built on ancient Simena (the name still commonly used today), it is another extremely pretty village with several good fish restaurants. At the top of the hill, reached by a steep climb, are the crenellated walls of a Byzantine fortress, enclosing a small Greek theatre.

The highlight is the Byzantine Batık Şehir (Sunken City), drowned after a massive earthquake. Remains are visible both above and below the water line, along the coast of

Above: *boatman amongst the submerged Lycian tombs of ancient Simena*

Kekova Island. Swimming is forbidden, but there are plenty of other excellent swimming and snorkelling stops, such as Tersane on Kekova Island, a small bay with a pebble beach, ruined Byzantine chapel and monastery. There are sea urchins, so wear shoes. Smaller boats may also go into a local sea cave.

KEMER ✪

As proud owner of one of the first stretches of really good beach west of Antalya, Kemer has become the hub of one of the most intensively developed stretches of the Turkish Riviera. The town itself is pleasantly small with enough Turkish people, supermarkets and orange groves to remind one of the real world. On the seafront, a host of hotels and restaurants and an aquapark line the little beach and smartly restored marina. There are also rapidly expanding strips of giant hotels at nearby Göynük, Beldibi, Çamyuva and Tekirova. There are, however, surprisingly few entertainments on offer locally; everything is provided by the all-inclusive resorts and many guests never leave their hotel grounds.

Below: *Kemer's marina is as crowded as its beaches with glamourous yachts from all around Europe*

➕ 28B2
✉ 45km southwest of Antalya on the N-400
ℹ Belediye ve Turizm Binası
   ☎ 0242-814 1112
🍴 Choice of restaurants (£)
🚌 *Dolmuş* from Antalya
♿ None
↔ Phaselis (➤ 26), Olympos (➤ 44), Antalya (➤ 53)

The Apple Blossom Tour

Distance
360km

Time
1 very full day; preferably 2 days. Go in Mar/Apr for blossoms. It is possible to stay overnight in Finike, but this is the last suitable point until you reach Antalya

Start/end point
Kemer
✚ 28B2

Lunch
At one of several small roadside restaurants near Arykanda, or at a café in Elmalı (£)

This magnificent circular drive encompasses all that is finest about Lycia. The first section, to Finike, follows the coast road; the next, as far as Elmalı, crosses the wild passes of the Taurus Mountains. The section from Elmalı to Korkuteli offers a rare glimpse of the high plains of inland Anatolia, and the last stretch to Antalya again meanders through forested mountains. There are numerous sights along the way, but the scenery is the real star. The tour is feasible in one day only if the more accessible sights are left for another occasion.

Leave Kemer on the N-400 heading south, past the turnings for Phaselis (➤ 26), Olympos and the Chimaera (➤ 44). At Finike (➤ 36), 71km from Kemer, turn on to the N-635 to Elmalı and Korkuteli.

Almost immediately, the coastal development gives way to peasant farms, with ramshackle old houses amongst the apple orchards and lemon groves, shaggy goats and chickens scratching in the verges, women in baggy trousers and cardigans working in the fields, and small flowery glades piled with beehives.

The 15th-century Ömerpaşa Camii in Elmalı has a finely tiled porch

After 7km, in Turunçova, turn right to Limyra (➤ 36), 3km off the main road. The signs peter out, but keep going as straight as possible. Just after you think you have taken a wrong turning, you see the first of the ruins. Return to the main road.

The main road continues north, past another group of rock tombs, winding along the milky turquoise Akçay river valley through spectacular pine-clad mountains. There are plenty of viewing points, but concentration is required, as brightly decorated fruit lorries tend to hurl themselves round the bends in a suicidal fashion.

After 21km, just beyond the pass, is the minute mountain village of Arif. Look out for a yellow

sign to Arykanda (► 32), hidden round a blind corner. The site is 1km off the main road along a rough track, just passable by car, with limited parking. To turn safely, go to the restaurant, turn round, then take the track on the left. If possible, leave your car at the restaurant and walk.
Back on the main road, keep going north through Göltana (a huge, shallow lake surrounded by snow-capped peaks in winter, a broad, dry pan in summer), for 38km to Elmalı.

Bees feast on the spring flowers to produce fine honey with rich overtones of Mediterranean herbs

This busy market town on the slopes of 2,296m Elmalı Dağ (literally 'mountain with apples') has a beautiful 15th-century mosque, the Ömerpaşa Camii, together with a number of fine, timber-framed Ottoman mansions. This is a crucially important area for Anatolian prehistory, with major Bronze Age settlements at nearby Karataş-Semayük and painted chamber tombs at Kızılbel and Karaburun, all within a 10km radius of the town. None are open to the public; the finds, including exquisite gold, silver and bronze jewellery and ivory figurines, are in the Antalya Archaeological Museum (Antalya Müzesi ► 17).

From Elmalı, head north to Korkuteli (52km), then turn right on to the N-350 past the Karain Cave (► 37) and Termessos (► 48) to Antalya (► 53–6), where you turn south, back on to the N-400 to Kemer (45km).

LETOÖN ✪✪

According to legend, the goddess Leto fled here from Mount Olympos to protect her twin babies, Apollo and Artemis, from Zeus's jealous wife, Hera. Local shepherds tried to drive her away, but she was aided by friendly wolves, in whose honour she changed the name of the area to Lycia (after *lykos*, the Greek word for wolf). She then turned the shepherds into frogs. Leto, Apollo and Artemis became the ruling deities of Lycia.

This charming little temple complex probably began as a site sacred to the Mother Goddess before the 7th century BC. It later became the place of assembly (parliament) of the Lycian federation. Today, there are three temples dedicated to Leto (2nd century BC, to the right), Artemis (4th or 5th century BC, in the centre) and Apollo (1st century BC, to the left), with a fine mosaic floor. Behind are a nymphaeum (fountain) and Byzantine basilica, in front various Roman buildings, including a small Hellenistic theatre. Many remain flooded for much of the year and are more like an aquarium than a Roman ruin, with huge numbers of frogs (shepherds?), terrapins, ducks and other water birds.

LİMYRA (FİNİKE, ➤ 36)

MARMARİS ✪✪

The huge, fjord-like bay at Marmaris, backed by steep, pine-clad mountains, once housed the ancient port of Physus. Little remains of this, but the natural deep-water harbour has attracted many notable sailors, including Süleyman the Magnificient who, in 1522, built a formidable, squat fortress (now an ethnographic museum) while preparing his successful attack on Rhodes. In 1798, Lord Nelson sheltered the British fleet here before defeating Napoleon in the Battle of the Nile. Marmaris is now a popular yachting centre, with a fabulous array of gin palaces next to the local *gülets*. The attractive town also has a pleasant seafront promenade and an excellent bazaar; the larger tourist hotels are strung out along the beach to the west. Better beaches are found at İçmeler (8km to the west) and Turunç (9km to the south).

Lying on the magnificently scenic peninsula west of Marmaris, along the N-400, are the popular little resort of Datça (76km) and the vast, largely unexcavated ruins of ancient Knidos (100km). The best way to visit is by boat.

28A1

✉ 26km west of Kalkan, off the N-400. The turn-off is 1.5km west of Kınık; the site is about 4km from the main road

🕐 May–Sep 7:30–7; Oct–Apr 8:30–5

🚌 *Dolmuş* to main road turn-off

♿ None, reasonable access

🎫 Cheap

↔ Kaş (➤ 21), Patara (➤ 23), Kalkan (➤ 37), Pınara (➤ 46), Saklıkent (➤ 47), Sidyma (➤ 47), Tlos (➤ 49), Xanthos (➤ 49)

28A2

✉ 146km west of Fethiye

ℹ İskele Meydanı 2

☎ 0252-412 1035

🚌 *Dolmuş* or coach

♿ None

🎫 All sights cheap

Alfresco dining – on the Marmaris waterfront – is one of the great treats of the Turkish coast

MYRA (DEMRE, ➤ 31)

ÖLÜDENİZ ✪✪✪

Freely acknowledged to be one of the most beautiful lagoons in the Mediterranean, Ölüdeniz (Dead Sea) was formed by a long spit of sand almost blocking off a circular bay. Steep, heavily forested mountains sweep down to the deep, blue water, while the sand spit provides acres of perfect sunbathing. Keep a close eye on children, as the sand of Belcekız Beach drops rapidly away from the shore and they could easily get into trouble in the deep water. The good news is that an area around the lagoon has been desig-nated a national park. The bad news is that it is a very small area; most of the sand spit is now a car park, the lagoon is filled with watersports and the whole valley leading down to the sea is wall-to-wall hotels and holiday homes. This has become one of the most crowded resorts in Turkey. If you like your beaches busy, this is definitely the place for you; if you like to admire the natural beauty in peace and quiet, come in January or look elsewhere.

🞧 28A2
✉ 17km south of Fethiye
🕐 Open access
🍴 Many restaurants and cafés in the village (££)
🚌 Dolmuş from Fethiye
♿ None
▥ Moderate
↔ Fethiye (➤ 35), Pınara (➤ 46), Saklıkent (➤ 47), Tlos (➤ 49)

Above: *the magnificent turquoise lagoon at Ölüdeniz is one of the finest sights of a spectacular coast*

Left: *antique and reproduction Ottoman coffee pots are sold in the Marmaris bazaar*

*Flames leap from the
ground at the
extraordinary Chimaera*

OLYMPOS AND THE CHİMAERA ✪✪✪

These linked sights – two of the most fascinating places on the Lycian coast – are hard to reach. From the main road, take the first (northerly) turning, just before the bridge, along a very twisty, narrow but utterly beautiful 9km road. Follow the increasingly rough dirt track through the village of Çıralı to the base of the hill, from where it is a 30-minute walk up to the Chimaera. It is possible to walk along the pebble beach between Çıralı and Olympos in summer (allow 15 minutes), but it involves fording a river on foot, so is not feasible in winter. The second direct access to Olympos, just beyond the bridge, is 8km from the main road, with a 3km dirt track at the end. It may not be passable in winter.

By the 2nd century BC, Olympos was one of the more important cities of the Lycian federation. Conquered by Cilician pirates in the 1st century BC, it was freed by Pompey in 67 BC and became part of the Roman Empire in AD 43. It was eventually abandoned after the Ottomans took control in the 15th century.

Today, it is a tranquil haven on the river mouth between high cliffs, filled with flowers, birds, frogs and even turtles. The partially excavated ruins cover an extraordinary range of history, from Lycian tombs near the harbour, to a Roman theatre and baths, a Byzantine basilica, and 11th- to 12th-century Genoese fortifications on the hill above.

The Chimaera (best seen at dusk) is a natural phenomenon: a series of flames spouting out of the bare hillside, thought to be fed by natural methane gas and named after the mythical monster said to inhabit these hills. According to Homer, she had the head of a lion, the torso of a goat and the tail of a serpent, and breathed fire. Bellerophon had to slay her to win the hand of the King of Lycia's daughter. Understandably, early Olympians worshipped Hephaestus (Vulcan), the god of fire, whose shrine stands near by. The Cilicians introduced the worship of Mithras, the Zoroastrian god of light, whose ceremonies also involved the flames. All of the surrounding mountains are part of the Beydağlar Olympos National Park, and there is plenty of good hiking.

PATARA (➤ 23, TOP TEN)

PHASELİS (► 26, TOP TEN)

PHELLOS ⭐

This almost entirely unexcavated site is one of the most remote and least known of all the ancient Lycian towns. To reach it, take the N-400 towards Finike for 10km, then turn on to the dirt road to Çukurbağ and continue up a driveable track for 5km until the road ends at the forest look-out station. It is then a 30-minute walk to the site. Stretches of fortified city wall are still standing, along with some vast, elaborate house tombs, the remains of a temple and some wells that are still in use. The mountain walk and the accompanying magnificent views are as much of an attraction as the ruins.

➕ 28B1
✉ About 20km north of Kaş
🕐 Open access
♿ None
🆓 Free
🔁 Kaş (► 21)

After the ruins, head for the beach at Olympos

PINARA

Another of the great cities of the Lycian federation, Pınara was probably founded as an off-shoot colony of Xanthos (➤ 49), some time in the 4th century BC. The ruins are scattered, unexcavated and overgrown, but the site is immensely dramatic, dominated by a sheer 500m red cliff. A difficult path leads to the top, where there are a few remains of the earliest town. The east face is honeycombed with often highly sophisticated Lycian tombs so inaccessible that their builders had to be lowered on ropes. The smaller hill to the east is the site of the later city. This also has a number of rock tombs, including the elaborate Royal Tomb, with reliefs depicting four walled cities and a festival. There are also an agora, temple and theatre.

RHODİAPOLİS

Reaching this remote site involves either an hour's walk through luscious mountain forests, or a four-by-four vehicle; the access track is not suitable for ordinary cars. For those with the time and energy, however, the walk is the biggest treat, the sight itself merely a goalpost. Using a local guide is sensible.

Rhodiapolis was a member of the Lycian federation. Sadly, its ruins, much damaged by vandals and fortune-hunters, are now scattered across the pine forest. At the centre is a well-preserved theatre; to the south are the ravaged remains of the vast, elaborate Tomb of Opramoas, a local philanthropist of note in the 2nd century AD. Measuring 8m by 7m, it was covered in sculpture and inscriptions recording the many honours bestowed on him for his charitable work throughout the Roman Empire.

---

*More Lycian rock tombs –
this time at Pinara*

SAKLIKENT ✪✪

This is where the Turks come to escape the gruelling heat in summer. The attraction is a cool, dark, narrow gorge, about 100m in height, carved out by the churning waters of the Eşen river. A wooden catwalk, starting modestly under the road bridge, leads into the dramatic gorge for about 150m; after that, those who are intrepid and wearing stout shoes, and who don't mind the water, can scramble on upstream. To cover the full length of the gorge requires the proper expeditionary equipment, organisation and mountaineering skills.

SIDYMA (DODURGA) ✪

Sidyma is a coastal city dating back to at least the 2nd century BC. Its ruins have been 'damaged' by locals being so unreasonable as to carry on living in the village, now called Dodurga. What traces of the Graeco-Roman settlement remain are scattered amongst the houses and across the surrounding hills. The mosque, built reusing ancient stones, has inscriptions to the pagan gods on the back wall. There is also a necropolis, a badly damaged theatre and a few remains of the agora and temple.

Did you know ?

The distinctive Lycian tombs (now all empty) were designed as family residences for the afterlife and probably closely mirrored domestic architecture of the period. Bodies were buried with a full range of possessions. In some cases, inscriptions give details of the inhabitants' lives, while the most important had relief carvings outside and frescoes inside.

➕ 28A1
✉ 44km east of Fethiye, off the N-350 to Korkuteli; 3km from main road
⊙ Open access
🍴 Several restaurants downstream (£–££)
♿ None
💲 Free
↔ Fethiye (➤ 35), Tlos, Xanthos (➤ 49)

➕ 28A1
✉ 29km north of Kalkan, about 7km off the N-400 to Fethiye (about 50km from Fethiye)
⊙ Open access
♿ None
💲 Free
↔ Patara (➤ 23), Letoön (➤ 42), Pınara (➤ 46), Xanthos (➤ 49)

Above: *The setting of Pınara theatre has as much drama as any performance on its stage*

Above: *magnificent views at Termessos*

 28B2

 37 km northwest of Antalya, off the N-350 to Korkuteli. Turn after 30km; the car park is about 9km from the main road up a forest track. Exploration involves a further, steep, 2km walk. Wear sensible shoes and take some water

Daily 8–7

Dolmuş to the turning off the main road

None, no access

Cheap

Antalya (➤ 53), Karain Mağarası (➤ 37), Apple Blossom Tour (➤ 40)

SİMENA (KEKOVA, ➤ 38)

TERMESSOS ✪✪✪

The city of Termessos, known as the 'Eagle's Nest', lies in a magnificent position, high in the mountains (1,650m), just within ancient Pisidia, guarding its borders with Lycia and Pamphylia.

The people of Termessos, fiercely warlike indigenous Anatolians, lived on the olive harvest and what they could take off others, both by demanding heavy tolls from passing travellers and a sideline in banditry. In 334 BC, they distinguished themselves by beating off Alexander, who was forced to raise the siege and move on after burning their olive groves. The city prospered during the Hellenistic years and from 70 BC to the 3rd century AD, retaining independence under Roman patronage. It was abandoned after a massive earthquake in AD 527. The rather overgrown ruins include a 4,200-seat theatre with a totally fabulous setting, the agora, a well-preserved Roman 'Founder's House', a colonnaded street, a gymnasium, an odeon, four temples, one dedicated to Zeus Solymeus, and a necropolis with nearly 1,000 tombs.

The surrounding area, including the dramatic Göksu Kanyon, is now protected from development as the Güllükdağı Termessos Milli Parkı (national park).

Nearby Döşmealtı village has a very high reputation as a weaving centre, producing magnificent carpets in strong, earthy colours and geometric designs.

TLOS

This is one of Lycia's longest inhabited cities, mentioned in 14th-century BC Hittite documents, whose Ottoman castle (built over the Lycian fortress) remained inhabited until the 19th century, when it was the haunt of the vicious pirate Kanlı Ali Ağa. The rock outcrop below the castle has numerous Lycian house tombs, including the elaborate Tomb of Bellerophon, slayer of the Chimaera (➤ 44), depicting the hero riding winged Pegasus. The local royal family claimed descent. The flatter land leading down to the Xanthos river was the site of a prosperous Roman city, whose remains include the agora, market hall, stadium, baths, a theatre, a Byzantine church and sections of the city wall.

28A2
36km east of Fethiye; turn off the N-350 to Korkuteli after 22km and follow signs to Yakaköy
Open access
None
Cheap
Kalkan (➤ 37), Kaş (➤ 21), Patara (➤ 23), Letoön (➤ 42), Pınara (➤ 46), Saklıkent (➤ 47), Sidyma (➤ 47), Xanthos (➤ 49)

Left: *only a few miles from the coast, ancient lifestyles continue*

Bottom left: *the wonderful theatre at Termessos is part of the landscape*

UÇAĞIZ (KEKOVA, ➤ 38)

XANTHOS

Xanthos was probably the single most important city in the Lycian federation. Its people had such overwhelming pride that twice in their history they totally destroyed the city rather than submit to a conqueror. In about 540 BC, when besieged by the Persian general Harpagos, the warriors slaughtered their families and slaves, then torched the city before the final battle. In 42 BC, when Roman Brutus arrived to collect funds for his war with Octavian and Mark Anthony, they did the same thing again. Only about 150 survived as captives. The following year, Mark Anthony helped them rebuild their city, which prospered as capital of Roman Lycia.

The ruins start partway up the hill with the 1st-century AD Arch of Vespasian, a Hellenistic gateway and the Nereid monument (about AD 4), now denuded of its decorative friezes. On the main outcrop stands a Roman theatre and agora and several pillar tombs, including a familiar Lycian tomb perched on a column, the 7.6m-high, 5th-century BC Harpy Tomb, with replica reliefs, and the Inscribed Pillar, recounting the life of a 5th-century BC prince, Kerei. On the acropolis behind are the remains of the earliest city, dating back to the 8th century BC, and a Byzantine monastery. The missing artwork was all removed by Sir Charles Fellows in 1838 and is now in the British Museum in London.

28A1
26km northwest of Kalkan. The turn-off is in the centre of Kınık town. The ancient site is about 1km from the turn-off, at the top of the hill
Open access; officially daily May–Oct 7:30–7; Nov–Apr 8–7:30
Café in the car park
Dolmuş to Kınık
None
Cheap
Kalkan (➤ 37), Kaş (➤ 21), Patara (➤ 23), Letoön (➤ 42), Pınara (➤ 46), Saklıkent (➤ 47), Sidyma (➤ 47), Tlos (➤ 49)

Food & Drink

Coffee

Coffee was introduced to the Turkish court in 1555 by two Syrian traders. By the late 17th century, the Sultan had his own coffee-maker, with 40 assistants, and the women in the harem were given intensive training in its preparation. It is an important element of hospitality: one local proverb says that 'a cup of coffee commits one to 40 years of friendship'. After finishing and draining your cup, you are said to be able to read your fortune in the coffee grounds.

Above: Turkish pastries are sticky, calorific and utterly delicious

Below: Turkish Delight, one of Turkey's most famous exports

With the growing popularity of the healthy Mediterranean diet, the basics of Turkish cuisine are surprisingly familiar to many visitors.

A typical meal begins with a choice of up to a dozen *meze* (*hors d'oeuvre*), including yoghurt with garlic and coriander; diced, fried liver; houmous (chickpea purée); various aubergine and spinach dishes, and *dolma* (vine leaves stuffed with rice, pine nuts, currants and herbs). With these comes the seemingly compulsory shepherd's salad, a sharply refreshing blend of tomato and cucumber, onion and green pepper, with a simple dressing of lemon and coriander.

Main Courses

Fundamental to the diet is the kebab, which comes in many guises: the *şişkebabı* (shish kebab), cubed lamb or chicken grilled on a skewer with pepper, onion and tomato; the *döner kebab*, the country's most popular form of fast food, with a huge joint or layered slab slowly spit-roasted and thinly sliced as required; the *köfte kebab*, flattened meatballs grilled on a skewer and served with a hot tomato sauce, and local specialities such as the hot *adaner kebab* – a long skewer wrapped in spicy minced lamb or goat.

Alternative main courses include simply grilled meat or fish and a variety of stews, most containing some of the key local ingredients of lamb, chicken, tomato, onion, peppers, aubergines, beans and chickpeas.

In the east, the bread is usually *pide*, a delicious pitta-style flat bread, sometimes served topped with vegetables or minced lamb as a type of pizza. Another common and delicious snack is *börek*, layers of thin pastry stuffed with minced lamb, cheese, spinach or other vegetables.

Puddings

Desserts are rare: the meal ends with fruit or simply with tea or coffee. Cakes, pastries and sweets abound, but are sold separately in pastry shops (*pastahanes*). Many are variations on the well-known *baklava*, flaky pastry filled with crushed nuts (pistachio, walnut or almond) and drenched in honey or syrup. There are also milky puddings such as *muhallabi* (rice pudding with cinnamon

and rose water) and *keşkül* (a paste of milk, ground almonds and pistachio, topped with coconut). In Antakya, the local speciality is *künefe*, a sweet, syrupy cheesecake (a cross between Welsh rarebit and *crème brûlée*). The most famous sweet is, of course, jellyish Turkish Delight (*lokum*), which comes flavoured with pistachio, lemon or rose-water.

Drinks

Alcohol is surprisingly free-flowing for a Muslim society, even away from the tourist areas. The local beer is a rather gassy lager, Efes, while the spirit of choice, *raki*, is an aniseed drink similar to ouzo or Pernod. There are some reasonable Turkish wines: most grapes are grown on the Aegean coast or in central Anatolia. The best names include Yakut, Villa Doluca and Dikmen.

Non-alcoholic options include fresh fruit juices and *ayran*, a thin, slightly salty yoghurt drink which is both refreshing and an excellent antidote to hot chillis. Tea (*çay*) or strong Turkish coffee (*kahve*) are both traditionally drunk black, strong and very sweet, in tiny glasses, as are various herbal or aromatic teas such as apple tea (*elma çay*), a favourite with tourists.

Top: *heaps of olives, feta cheese and tiny glasses of tea – key ingredients of Turkish cuisine*

Above: *sun-ripened peaches, fresh from the tree*

51

Pamphylia

It is hard to imagine today, but in 500 BC Pamphylia, ruled from Side, was the poorest and least significant of the three kingdoms that stretched along the Mediterranean coast. Its wealth grew when the Romans poured money into the architectural infrastructure of Perge and Aspendos. Today, its coffers are filled by large expanses of beach-lined coastal plain, ideal for large-scale tourist development. A building boom has thrown up whole new resorts, with scattered hotels creeping together to form unbroken lines many miles long.

Pamphylia's western border is marked by Antalya, southern Turkey's tourist capital, fringed by the 12km-long hotel strip of Lara. At its eastern edge stand Alanya and the parade of giant resorts at İncekum. Between them are the three great ancient settlements of Perge, Aspendos and Side. The coastal scenery is duller than Lycia's, but the driving is easier, there are long, golden beaches and inland are the mountainous delights of the Köprülü Kanyon.

> '*This country... is one of the finest regions of the world.*'
>
> IBN BATTUTA, Arab traveller
> (1325–1354)

Antalya

Ever since Antalya was built, travellers such as the 14th-century Arab explorer, Ibn Battuta, the 19th-century British sea captain, Francis Beaufort, and 1950s explorer, Freya Stark, have praised its outstanding beauty.

Originally known as Attaleia, the city was founded in 158 BC by King Attalus II of Pergamon, who needed a sea outlet for his various territories. The only suitable city, Side, was protected by Rome and beyond his grasp. Antalya too became Roman, bequeathed to the empire by Attalus III in 133 BC; it then came under Byzantine control, and was used as a staging post by the Crusaders until it was eventually conquered by the Selçuks in 1206. In the 1390s, it was transferred to the Ottomans and remained their property until 1918, when it was given to Italy in the post-war carve-up of the empire. Only three years later, Atatürk threw out all foreigners, but the Italians had already imbued the city with an elegance and dedication to the good life. Today, Antalya has a population of over one million, a busy port and a dynamic tourist resort. Its setting is magnificent, tucked into a bowl surrounded by the snow-capped peaks of the Taurus Mountains and fronted by a long, curving bay and deep turquoise sea. The outskirts are a grim concrete sprawl, but the old city centre is beautiful, having enjoyed lavish restoration in the 1980s.

The only proper beach is the crowded shingle Konyaaltı Beach, west of the old town. The most popular beaches are Büyük Çaltıcak and Küçük Çaltıcak, 10 to 12km west.

Antalya harbour, once the pride of the Ottomans, is now a tourist jewel of the Turkish Riviera

What to See in Antalya

ANTALYA MÜZESİ (► 17, TOP TEN)

KALEİÇİ

In 1671, Turkish traveller Evliya Çelebi described the city of Antalya as being totally surrounded by a wall 4,400m long, with 80 towers and four gates. Inside it was divided into four quarters, accessed by a further 22 gates, each containing 1,000 houses. One quarter was for the Greeks, one for the Jews, one for the Muslims, and one for the king, his court and the Mamelukes (ruling class).

In the early 1980s, the old walled town of Kaleiçi (meaning citadel) was spectacularly redeveloped. The main docks had long since moved to Setur, 10km west, and the harbour was now converted to a glitzy marina, its quay lined with restaurants. At the far western end is a small, modern amphitheatre, used for live performances in summer. Above, hundreds of Ottoman houses have been saved and restored. The best way to explore the steep, narrow streets is on foot. Start at the top and work down to the harbour, where there are plenty of cafés and taxis to take the faint-hearted back uphill.

- 28B2
- Open access
- Choice of cafés, bars and restaurants (£–£££)
- Dolmuş, taxi
- None; streets steep
- Free

Heavily fortified walls protect Antalya's old harbour, now a marina for pleasure boats and yachts

About halfway down on the right is the Yivli Minare (Fluted Minaret, ► 56). A little further down, on the left, you will find the Karatay Medrese (religious school), which was built in 1250 by a Selçuk vizier. Currently undergoing restoration, it has a beautifully carved triumphal entrance.

At the eastern end of the quay, a quick but brutal flight of stairs climbs the cliff, from where a path leads to the mysterious Hıdırlık Kulesi, a 13.45m round tower squatting on a square base at the harbour entrance. Built in the 2nd century AD, it has been described variously as a lighthouse, a fort and also a tomb.

Behind this, Hesapçi Sok heads straight into the old residential area, a maze of tiny streets and alleys overhung by rickety wooden-frame houses. A few blocks up on the right is the ruined Kesik Minare Camii (Mosque of the Truncated Minaret), a 13th-century mosque, converted from a 5th-century AD Byzantine church built on the site of a Roman temple. In 1851, a lightning strike and fire gave the mosque its name.

A couple of blocks further, on the right, is the Suna-İnan Kıraç (► 56). Hadrian's Gate in Atatürk Caddesi is a stately marble triple arch built to welcome the Emperor Hadrian in AD 130; it marks the eastern edge of Kaleiçi.

Restored Ottoman houses in Kaleiçi, with formidable walls surrounding courtyard gardens

There are excellent views of the old town's painted roofs and the sparkling harbour below from Kalekapısı Square, site of the Clock Tower. This was built in 1244 as part of the main city fortifications, and is now one of Antalya's best-known landmarks. It's an excellent aid to navigation, standing right in the heart of the city at the entrance to the old town. Beside it, to the left, is the 18th-century Tekeli Mehmet Paşa Camii (mosque). To the right, on Cumhuriyet Square, is the magnificent Atatürk Monument. Every town in Turkey has a compulsory statue dedicated to the great leader: Antalya has two and this is one of Turkey's finest.

Old and new symbols of a city: Antalya's memorial to Atatürk in front of the Yivli Minare

🛉 28B2
✉ Barbaros Mah, Kocatepe Sok 25, Kaleiçi
☎ 0242-243 4274
🕐 Thu–Tue 9–6. Closed Wed
🍴 Café in the museum, many restaurants and cafés near by (£–£££)
♿ None
💵 Moderate

🛉 28B2
✉ Kaleiçi
🕐 Daily 8:30–5
🚌 Clock Tower
♿ None; reasonable access
💵 Free
↔ Kaleiçi (➤ 54–5)

SUNA-İNAN KİRAÇ (RESEARCH INSTITUTE) ✪✪

Two beautiful buildings, a two-storey Ottoman mansion and the Greek church of Agios Georgios (St George), behind it, have been impeccably restored and opened as a specialist research institute, library and archive for the study of the archaeology, history, ethnography and culture of Mediterranean civilisations. There is also exhibition space for items from the Kiraç's extensive collection, and regular changing exhibitions of anything from ceramics to maps. Well worth a visit.

YİVLİ MİNARE (FLUTED MINARET) ✪✪

Selçuk Sultan Alâeddin Keykubad I (1219–38) was the single greatest builder along the Mediterranean coast, responsible for many fine buildings, including the Alanya Citadel (➤ 16), Alarahan caravansaray (➤ 61) and this beautiful mosque (built in 1230), which has become the symbol of Antalya. The 38m-high brick minaret, with eight fluted sections on a stone base, was lavishly decorated with turquoise and dark blue tiles. It stands in the grounds of a mosque built in 1373 by Mehmet Bey. Beside it, a very old olive tree has grown up over the grave of a wise *muezzin*. It is customary to write a wish on a slip of paper, wrap it in an olive leaf and put it into the hollow trunk. (They do, of course, come true.)

Alanya

The first real documentation of Alanya comes in 197 BC, when the settlement, then known as Coracesium, was besieged by Antiochus III of Syria. In the next century, a pirate chief, Diodotus Tryphon, overthrew the Syrians and built the fortress to use as his base. Eventually, the activities of the pirates provoked Rome into action; Pompey was dispatched to sort them out, and Coracesium joined the empire. During the Byzantine era, the city changed its name to Kalonoros ('beautiful mountain'), changing again in 1221, when it was ceded to Selçuk Sultan Alâeddin Keykubad I, who renamed it Alaiye (city of Ala), after himself. The city grew and flourished around his extraordinary citadel (► 16), its star only fading after it was captured by the Ottomans in 1471.

🕇 28C2
✉ 135km east of Antalya
🍴 Choice of restaurants (£–£££)
🛈 Damlataş Mağarasi Yanı, Damlataş Cad 1
☎ 0242-513 1240
🚌 *Dolmuş* stop on the seafront opposite Damlataş Cave
♿ Few; reasonable access
↔ Anamur (► 22) Alarahan (► 61), Side (► 68)

Above: *modern Alanya curls around a sweeping bay*

Below: *Alanya's busy beach*

Today, Alanya has a small, very run-down, half-ruinous old town within the outer walls of the citadel; a thriving tourist zone around the charming old harbour, with brash modern hotels stretching along the beaches to east and west, and a busy, entirely Turkish city inland.

The 3km beach, west of town, is the city's own main beach; the 8km to the east are largely fronted by resort hotels. Both have grey-brown sand, but are otherwise good, clean and usually crowded. The best beach in the area, at İncekum, about 20km west, is lined with huge resorts, which offer a range of watersports and other activities. There is almost nothing outside the hotels, apart from a couple of second-rate cafés and a few shops.

A Walk Around Alanya

Distance
About 7km

Time
Allow 2 hours

Start point
Beside the entrance to the İç Kale
✚ 28C2
🚌 *Dolmuş* or taxi

End point
Beside Damlataş Cave
✚ 28C2
🚌 *Dolmuş* or taxi

Lunch
At any of several harbour-front cafés; there are also plenty of drinks stops *en route* (£)

Most of this walk from the İç Kale (➤ 16) is down a steep hill, accessible to all of average fitness but hard on the knees. Anyone who tires *en route* can simply stop and flag down the next *dolmuş* or taxi.

Follow the hairpin bends of the main road down, keeping to the side (there are no pavements and you will be invisible to cars).

After about 1.5km, a fork to the right leads to a viewing point, where you can look out over the harbour, below.

After 1km more, a path on the left leads to the ruins of the ancient city.

Meander around the narrow alleys, before taking one of three routes back to the main road. Look out for the city entrance arch; two old mosques: the Akşebe Türbesi (1230), containing the tomb of its founder, Akşebe Sultan, and the Süleymaniye Mosque (1231), reconstructed in the 16th century during the reign of Süleyman the Magnificent; and the 13th-century caravansaray, now the Bedesten Hotel.

Pizza on the pavement in holiday Alanya

After another 1.5km, at the edge of the modern town, choose one of the narrow streets heading downhill on the harbour side; you will eventually come out near the Kızıl Kule (➤ 59). Walk around the harbour to the main street of cafés opposite the tour boats then turn left and walk through the modern town along flat, easy Damlataş Street, or along the smaller Sultan Alâeddin Street, both of which come out next to the museum and tourist office.

What to See in Alanya

ALANYA MÜZESİ (ALANYA MUSEUM)

There are only two display rooms in this well-presented little museum. The first covers the history of the region with a broad range of exhibits, including Hittite sculpture, Bronze Age pottery, coins from early Coracesium, Greek and Roman statues and glass. The second room is the ethnographic section, with carpets, costumes, gold and silver jewellery and a reconstructed Turkish living room. The garden has a variety of mainly Roman sculptures, urns and sarcophagi.

> ✚ 28C2
> ✉ Azaklar Sok
> ☎ 0242-513 1228
> 🕐 Tue–Sun, 8–12, 1:30–5:30
> 🍴 Moderate
> 🚌 *Dolmuş* stop on the seafront opposite Damlataş Cave
> ♿ None; access reasonable

DAMLATAŞ MAĞARASI (WEEPING CAVE) ✪

This small seaside cave complex has two accessible chambers, both surrounded by wonderful curtains of strangely formed stalactites and stalagmites. The air is warm, thick and humid: 90 to 100 per cent humidity, at a constant temperature of 22–3°C, with high levels of carbon dioxide, natural ionisation and radiation. Sufferers of asthma and rheumatism come here for a cure, which involves sitting in the cave four hours a day for 21 days: it's said to have an 80 per cent success rate.

> ✚ 28C2
> ✉ South end of western beach
> 🕐 Daily 10–8; open to people taking the cure 6AM–10AM
> 🍴 Cheap
> 🚌 *Dolmuş* stop on the seafront opposite Damlataş Cave
> ♿ None; no access

İÇ KALE (INNER CITADEL, ► 16, TOP TEN)

KIZIL KULE (RED TOWER) ✪✪✪

This formidable 35m octagonal tower was designed in 1227 by a Syrian architect for Sultan Alâeddin Keykubad I, as the first line of defence of the Alanya harbour and citadel (► 16). With its thick, red-brick walls, arrow slits and troughs for pouring boiling water, tar or oil on to attackers, it follows classic medieval castle design. Inside, each of the five storeys has eight sections of arched galleries surrounding a vast water cistern.

> ✚ 28C2
> ✉ Eastern harbour
> 🕐 Daily 10–8
> ♿ None

Fully restored in 1951, the tower now contains a small ethnographic museum with attractive displays of carpets and costumes, a few carved wooden panels and wonderful views from the battlements. The steps are extremely steep and unprotected in places so be very careful when making the ascent.

Kızıl Kule guards the fishing boats in Alanya harbour

Alanya Harbour Boat Trip

Alanya harbour is lined with *gülets*, all competing to take you on a trip around the harbour or down the coast.

The boat pulls away, giving an excellent view of the city and Kızıl Kule (➤ 59). It heads out past a series of five huge open workshops with arched roofs.

These are the Tersane, the last remaining Selçuk dockyard in Turkey, built by Sultan Alâeddin Keykubad I in about 1227 to service his navy. Continuing round the point, the Tophane Kule (Arsenal Tower) was built for defence, also in the 13th century, but was used as a cannon foundry in Ottoman times.

The boat passes under the citadel and cliff.

Alanya harbour is still used by jazzy local fishing boats

Time
Allow 1 or 2 hours (recommended) for harbour tours; there are also half and full-day trips.

Start and end points
Alanya harbour
➕ 28C2

Lunch
Usually provided for day trips; soft drinks on shorter trips.

The most dramatic element of the harbour tour is this magnificent red cliff, topped by the even more imposing curtain wall of the citadel (➤ 16): this is one of the best ways of experiencing its true size. A small opening in the cliff-face marks the bottom of an escape tunnel, leading right up into the castle. Further on, the agile and thin may be offered the chance to leap into a tiny tunnel leading right through the peninsula, then make the nerve-wracking jump back on to a wildly rocking boat.

Longer trips also involve stops at a series of sea caves.

These intriguing places include the shining Fosforlu (Phosphorus Cave), the Aşıklar Mağarası (Lovers' Cave), where a couple supposedly survived for three months in 1965, the Korsanlar Mağarası (Pirates' Cave) and Cleopatra's Beach, where legend says the great queen used to swim.

What to See in Pamphylia

ALARAHAN ✪✪

Set in a charming valley, next to a tumbling river, this is one of the coast's best-preserved caravansaray, built in 1232 by Sultan Alâeddin Keykubad I as part of a country-wide network of travellers' hostels. Unusually, it was also used as a dervish monastery.

Entirely roofed, the building has a central communal area in which the travellers ate and conversed, surrounded by small side rooms for sleeping. These all have small windows looking out into the broad, vaulted corridors used as servants' quarters and stables (to allow the master to keep an eye on his possessions). To the left of the entrance is a fountain, to the right a small mosque.

High on the mountain above is a dramatic fortress. No one knows its true origin, but it was rebuilt and used by the Selçuks to protect travellers. Behind it is a rare painted bath house. Access involves a serious climb. Whitewater rafting is available from the restaurant opposite.

28C2

38km west of Alanya; turn off the N-400 after 30km

Open access

Restaurants opposite (£)

Dolmuş

None, but some access to the caravansaray

Free

Alanya (➤ 57–60), Manavgat (➤ 67), Side (➤ 68)

Above: the Selçuk Alara fortress was built to protect the mountain passes

ASPENDOS (► 18, TOP TEN)

BELEK

Belek doesn't yet appear on most tourist maps. There is a small village somewhere, among the low-rise apartment blocks, but the name is used for a major new resort area south of Aspendos. Inland accommodation and facilities seem distinctly down-market, but there is a splendid beach, shared by the local turtles and a row of giant resort hotels. Belek is also the home of Turkey's premier golf course, within a stone's throw of Antalya airport.

✚ 28C2
✉ About 38km east of Antalya, off the N-400; turn off after 31km
🍽 Choice of restaurants in Aspendos (££)
🚌 *Dolmuş* to turn-off
♿ None
↔ See Aspendos (► 18)

Did you know ?

The loggerhead turtle, Caretta caretta, *nests on 17 beaches in Turkey. Each year, between May and October, the turtles return to their home beach to breed. Born in darkness, the babies have to make a perilous 15-minute dash for the safety of the water. Beach umbrellas can crush the nests, while a light at night can disorientate the infants and send them in the wrong direction.*

BURDUR

Directly north of Antalya, across the bulk of the Taurus Mountains, is an area of huge natural lakes. Burdur Gölü is a shallow salt lake covering some 200sq km, surrounded by scrub. There are several excellent bathing beaches, including the 5km-long Çendik Beach (2km from town). Burdur town, on the eastern shore, has a 14th-century mosque, the Ulu Cami, and a small museum, housed in the Ottoman Bulgurlu Medrese, containing many finds from nearby Kremna (► 66) and Hacılar, a rich prehistoric archaeological site dating back to the 6th millennium BC.

✚ 28B2
✉ 104km north of Antalya, on the N-650
ℹ Burç Mah, Cumhuriyet Meydanı, Kültür Sarayı, Kat 2
🕐 Museum: Tue–Sun 9:30–12, 1:30–5:30
💰 Museum: cheap

Burdur has incorporated ancient friezes into modern buildings

DÜDEN ŞELÂLESİ (DÜDEN FALLS) ✪

The area around Antalya is limestone country, whose remote hills are littered with karst springs, sinkholes, underground rivers and waterfalls. Born of an underground river, the Düden Falls are a powerful and beautiful series of cascades crashing through a narrow gorge. The Upper Falls are a popular local picnic spot, with steps leading down to a soggy but very pretty walkway behind the curtain of water. The surrounding park seethes with bodies in high summer. The 20m Lower Düden Falls gush straight over the cliff into the sea, and are best seen from a boat, which can tuck right in under the spray in a whirl of rainbows. They are included on most *gület* trips from Antalya harbour.

EĞİRDİR ✪✪

Built on the loveliest of the Pisidian lakes (and the second largest freshwater lake in Turkey), Eğirdir is the prettiest of the local towns. It was founded by Hittites, and has been a tourist resort since the 5th century BC, a popular stopover on the King's Way, between Ephesus and Babylon. In the Middle Ages, it became the local capital of the Hamidoğlu dynasty, and still has a rich, atmospheric collection of old Greek and Ottoman houses spilling off the small peninsula on to two tiny islands linked by causeways. The town has a ruined Selçuk fort and a 15th-century mosque, the Hızırbey Camii. Next door, the Dündar Bey Medrese (1218) is now a shopping mall. The Thursday market is excellent and there are several good beaches near by, the best of them at Bedre Köyü, 8km out of town on the Barla road.

✚ 28B2
✉ Upper Falls, Kızılırmak Caddesi, off the northern by-pass,14km northeast of Antalya; Lower Falls about 10km east of Antalya, near Lara Beach
⊙ Open access
🍴 Cafés and restaurants near the Upper Falls (££)
♿ None
🖐 Free
↔ Antalya (➤ 53–6)

✚ 28B2
✉ 86km northeast of Burdur via the N-685 and N-330
ℹ 2 Sahil Yolu 13
☎ 0246-311 4388
🍴 Choice of *pansiyons* and restaurants on the islands and waterfront (££)
🚌 *Dolmuş*
♿ None

Above: *the lower Düden Falls plunge straight into the sea*

İNCEKUM (ALANYA, ➤ 57)

KOCAİN MAĞARASI (KOCAIN CAVE) ✪

This is the largest cave in Turkey, discovered in 1919 by an Italian caver, Guiseppe Moretti: it has an entrance 18m high and 74m across, leading into a vast cavern 633m deep and 35m high. Inside, immediately to the right of the entrance, is an altar; to the left are some Greek inscriptions. These, together with a huge water cistern, suggest that the cave was used as a church by early Christians. Further in, there are massive pillar stalactites, 8m in diameter and 35m long. There are plans to open the cave for organized tours, but for the present, you are on your own. If you wish to explore, take a powerful torch, good boots and some drinking water.

KÖPRÜLÜ KANYON/SELGE ✪✪✪

The prosaically named 'Canyon with a Bridge' is one of the most enchanting stretches of country in Pamphylia. Allow plenty of time for a leisurely meal of freshly tickled trout, a long country walk and the compulsory old stones at Selge.

From the turn-off, a good road winds up through the forested foothills into the Taurus Mountains, the air cooling noticeably as you reach a height of about 1,000m; much of the way, the road follows the Köprü Irmağı valley. At the end of the tarmac road (43km) is a cluster of restaurants and the base camp of many whitewater rafting companies. A short distance up the hill, take the left-hand fork of the now gravel road, which crosses a beautiful single-arched Roman stone bridge, high above the gorge. Park just beyond this and walk down to the left for about 1km, along the rim of the canyon, to a second Roman bridge. Follow the road to the right, as it heads up higher still, climbing 700m on to the plateau and after 14km reaching the village of Altınkaya (Zerk) and the ruins of ancient Selge, once a Pisidian city of 20,000 people. Although the road deteriorates and is precipitous in places, it is still driveable with care, and there are fabulous views across the wild valleys. As you get near, look out for the 'fairy chimneys', extraordinary wind-carved columns of soft volcanic rock.

The path leads through the village, which is totally entangled with the ancient city, whose marble columns double as fence posts and garden furniture. It brings you out at the back of a magnificent Greek-style theatre set against a backdrop of snow-capped mountains. From here, a path leads along the Roman main street to the agora and a Byzantine basilica. Beyond this are the remains of twin temples to Artemis and Zeus.

⊞ 28B2
✉ 50km north of Antalya; take the Burdur road for 27km, then turn off and continue to the village of Ahırtaş, from where there is a two-hour walk up to the cave
🕓 Open access
🚌 *Dolmuş* to Ahırtaş
♿ None
🎫 Free

⊞ 28C2
✉ About 99km east of Antalya; turn off the N-400 about 47km east of Antalya (just past Aspendos), 28km west of Side
🕓 Open access
🍴 Numerous restaurants along the river (£)
🚌 *Dolmuş*
♿ None
🎫 Canyon free; Selge cheap (if the guard is there)
↔ Antalya (➤ 17 and 53–6), Aspendos (➤ 18), Perge (➤ 24–5), Kurşunlu Şelâlesi (➤ 67), Side (➤ 68), Sillyon (➤ 69)

Opposite: *Köprülü Kanyon, a major excavation by a small but determined river*

28B2

About 115km north of
Antalya, off the N650:
5km before Buçak, turn
right through Çamlık to
Kremna (8km)

Open access

Dolmuş

None

Cheap (if guard is there)

KREMNA

The recently excavated Pisidian city of Kremna stands in a spectacular location on a clifftop promontory overlooking the Aksu river. It seems to have been one of the more modern cities in the region, but was certainly flourishing by the 5th century BC. From the late 1st century BC, it came under the direct control of the Roman Empire, and its defensive walls were built. Over a century later, under Hadrian, came a major rebuilding which gave it a grand 230m-long colonnaded street, forum, monumental staircase, propylon, bath house and theatre. More interesting, perhaps, are the remains of war. In AD 270, the city was seized by a local brigand, Lydius, and the Romans had to wage a prolonged siege to get their city back. Archaeologists have found not only various weapons, including artillery, missiles and huge stones for rolling on to the enemy, but the remains of a siege mound (a ramp built under the walls by the Romans). Finds are in Burdur Museum (➤ 62).

KURŞUNLU ŞELÂLESİ (KURŞUNLU FALLS)

This is a pleasant, brief stop with high waterfalls plunging into a bubbling pool, surrounded by wooded cliffs and a small, very organised national park. Outside, there are decorative camels for expensive rides and exorbitant pictures, a huge car park and souvenir stalls. Inside, the cool, shady park has a children's playground, picnic tables and carefully marked walks to the falls and along the river.

✚ 26B2
✉ 23km east of Antalya, 7km off main road
🕐 Daily 8.30–5.30
🍴 Drink and snack stands (£)
🚐 *Dolmuş*
👟 Moderate, parking fee

MANAVGAT

Manavgat is much larger and busier than neighbouring Side (➤ 68), but has little to hold the attention other than boat trips upstream to the Manavgat Şelalesi, an attractive waterfall 3km north of the town, surrounded by pleasant gardens, a good restaurant and tatty souvenir shops. The remote and virtually unknown ancient city of Seleukeia, with the remains of its city gate, bath, agora, market hall and temple, is an hour's mountain hike away.

✚ 28C2
✉ 5km east of Side
🕐 Open access
🍴 Restaurants in Manavgat (££); take refreshments if walking to Seleukeia
🚐 *Dolmuş*
♿ None
👟 Free
🔁 Side (➤ 68)

PERGE (➤ 24, TOP TEN)

SAGALASSOS

Built on the steep, rocky slope of 2,000m Mount Akdağ, about 1,500m above sea level, dramatically sited Sagalassos was one of the most important Pisidian cities. Captured with difficulty by Alexander, it was eventually to become Roman, but always retained a great degree of independence. The few excavated ruins from the Hellenistic period include a *heroön* (heroic shrine), decorated with a frieze of dancers (now in the village), a Doric temple, as well as a nymphaeum, bouleterion (council hall) and a potters' quarter with literally thousands of abandoned pots. Roman remains are far more extensive and include a restored agora, odeon, baths, several temples, a theatre and a colonnaded street.

✚ 28B2
✉ About 25km east of Burdur, off the N-685 to Isparta, through the village of Ağlasun
🕐 Open access
♿ None
👟 Cheap (when guard is present)

The Manavgat Falls are a popular picnic place for local Turks escaping the searing summer heat

67

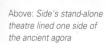

Above: *Side's stand-alone theatre lined one side of the ancient agora*

Right: *the dramatically sited columns of Apollo's temple at Side*

Bottom right: *sunset ride along the beach at Side*

✚ 28C2

✉ 72km east of Antalya; turn off the N-400 3km west of Manavgat

☎ 0242-753 1265

🍴 Choice of restaurants (£–£££)

🚌 Dolmuş

ℹ Side Yolu Üzeri; off the main road, about 1km north of the town centre

♿ None

↔ Antalya (► 17, 53–6), Aspendos (► 18), Perge (► 24), Köprülü Kanyon (► 64), Kurşunlu Şelâlesi (► 67), Sillyon (► 69)

SİDE ✪✪✪

Side should be the perfect holiday destination. It is a delightfully pretty little town, built on a peninsula lined with long, gold sand beaches, with attractive old houses, waterfront restaurants and a harbour filled with sleek yachts and jazzy fishing boats. Even better, the modern town is built among the ruins of the ancient city, so sightseeing involves only a gentle stroll. In winter, it is idyllic. But Side is a victim of its own success. Rampant development has given the tiny town a staggering 25,000 hotel beds. In season, the good shops are surrounded by tat, too many of the restaurants drip neon and belt out the decibels and the beaches and cafés are packed.

Ancient Side ('pomegranate' in Anatolian) was founded in the 7th century BC and, courtesy of a roaring trade in slaves, sharp practice and piracy, grew into the richest port on the Pamphylian coast. It was torched by Arab invaders in the 10th century AD and finally abandoned after an earthquake in about 1150. Cretan Muslim fishermen resettled here early in the 20th century, survived Atatürk's exchange of population and are now raking it in.

The approach road passes through the Hellenistic city gate, where long stretches of the city walls and aqueduct are visible. A few hundred metres on are the agora (probably the site of the slave market) and imposing free-standing theatre (on the left). Beside the agora are the semicircular remains of a 24-seat public lavatory. Beyond it, a path leads to a second agora, a Byzantine basilica and an episcopal palace, and over the dunes and city wall to the beach. On the opposite side of the road, the 3rd-century AD bath house is now home to a fine **museum**.

The main road passes through a narrow 4th-century AD monumental arch (on a blind corner), beside which stands an elaborate nymphaeum (fountain) honouring emperors Titus and Vespasian. It then follows the course of the old Roman road through the town to the harbour. On the headland to the left, a few elegantly placed columns are all that remain of the temples of Apollo and Athena.

SİLLYON ✪

Sillyon's 200m-high, flat-topped acropolis is a landmark for miles around. Founded in around 1200 BC, this was a thriving city long before Alexander tried – and failed – to capture it in 333 BC. It continued to flourish throughout the Roman era.

The lower path passes the stadium, Hellenistic lower gate and gymnasium, later used as a Byzantine bishops' palace. From here, a heavily buttressed ramp leads past the 3rd to 6th-century BC necropolis to the Upper Gate. Within the walls are many Hellenistic structures, including several large public buildings, private houses, an odeon, a temple, numerous large and dangerously unmarked water cisterns and the remnants of a theatre. Nearly half the ruins were scattered across the plain below during a massive landslide in 1969.

Museum and Archaeological Site

- ⊠ On the main road at the entrance to the town
- ☎ 0242-753 1006
- 🕔 Museum: Tue–Sun 8–12, 1–5. Closed Mon. Archaeological site: open access; theatre currently closed for restoration
- 🎟 Museum: cheap; archaeological site: free
- ❓ Paid car park for museum and archaeological site further up the hill, through the arch

---

- ✚ 28B2
- ⊠ About 33km east of Antalya. Turn off the N-400 after 25km and follow the side road for 8km to Asar Köyü; steep climb up unmarked dirt track to site
- 🕔 Open access
- ⓹ None
- 🎟 Free; use of a local guide recommended
- ↔ Antalya (➤ 17 and 53–6), Aspendos (➤ 18), Perge (➤ 24), Köprülü Kanyon (➤ 64), Kurşunlu Şelâlesi (➤ 67), Side (➤ 68)

In the Know

If you only have a short time to visit the Turkish Coast, or would like to get a real flavour of the region, here are some ideas:

10
Ways to Be a Local

Shake hands and spend a few minutes making small talk before getting down to business.

Learn a few words of Turkish; your efforts will be greatly appreciated.

Take off your shoes on entering a mosque or private house.

Accept a second glass of tea if offered; to refuse implies that the first was below standard.

Women should cover their heads, and both sexes should cover shoulders and knees when entering a mosque.

Lift your head backwards to say no, nod down for yes, shake it from side to side if you don't understand.

Do not point your finger, kiss or hug anyone of the opposite sex or blow your nose in public.

Never lose your temper or shout at anyone; to lose control is to lose respect.

Turks are immensely patriotic; don't mock Turkey, Islam or Atatürk.

Staring, standing close and touching you when talking is acceptable and normal behaviour; a few men push their luck (you will know the difference).

10
Good Places to Have Lunch

• Eat fish you caught that morning at a beach barbecue on Kekova Island (➤ 38).

• Relax on a sunny harbourfront terrace overlooking the fishing boats in Side (➤ 68).

• Eat freshly caught trout beside a mountain river at Saklıkent (➤ 47) or Köprülü Kanyon (➤ 64).

• Attack the buffet on a gently rocking *gület* after spending an hour snorkelling in turquoise waters.

• Picnic on the beach, under a shady pine tree, propped against a Lycian harbour wall at Phaselis (➤ 26).

• Unwind at a roadside restaurant on the Anamur–Silifke road, its terrace jutting dizzyingly over the the cliff (➤ 71, 10 Great Roads).

• Have a *döner kebab* and a glass of *ayran* in a simple backstreet café, surrounded by Turkish men chain-smoking black tobacco.

• Picnic on a mountain top overlooking the sea and

A fine Turkish carpet is a work of art and heirloom of the future

terraced valleys at St Simeon's Monastery (➤ 90).

• Share a *pide* with the village women, crouched around the fire as they prepare the evening meal.

• Splurge at one of the elegant battlement restaurants in Antalya old town (➤ 54–5).

10
Top Activities

• Diving
• Four by four jeep safaris
• Golf
• Mountain biking
• Rafting
• Riding
• Sailing
• Skiing
• Trekking
• Water-skiing, windsurfing and other watersports

10
Top Beaches

• Alanya (➤ 57)
• Belek, near Aspendos (➤ 62)
• Göynük, near Kemer (➤ 39)
• İncekum, near Alanya (➤ 57)
• İztuzu, near Dalyan (➤ 34)
• Marmaris (➤ 42)
• Ölüdeniz, near Fethiye (➤ 43)
• Patara (➤ 23)
• Phaselis (➤ 26)
• Side (➤ 68)

10
Great Roads

These are all chosen for their magnificent scenery. The driving is therefore extremely difficult; be very cautious.

Right: *local women work together in the open*

• 12km loop around the peninsula in Kaş (➤ 21).
• 18km coast road between Finike and Demre (➤ 36 and 31).
• 66km mountain road from Finike to Elmalı (➤ 40–1).
• 52km plains road between Elmalı and Korkuteli (➤ 40–1).
• 8km road through the woods to Çıralı and the Chimaera (➤ 44).
• Dramatic 75km stretch from Gazipaşa to Anamur, with 1,000m-high cliffs (➤ 78).

Water slides and plenty of bronzed bodies at an Antalya water park

• Towering seacliff road from Anamur to Silifke (about 50km of a 143km journey; ➤ 78 and 86).
• 49km main highway south from İskenderun to Antakya (➤ 80–2 and 84).
• Rough 20km round trip up to St Simeon's monastery, near Antakya (➤ 90).
• 57km stretch from the main road to Köprülü Kanyon and Selge (➤ 64).

Cilicia &
the Hatay

Most of the landscape in this easternmost section of the Turkish coast is less than inspiring: a broad plain with heavily industrialised cities such as Adana and İskenderun. But the area around Antakya is attractive, and the coast between Alanya and Silifke is spectacular.

Cilicia (roughly Alanya to Adana) was once part of the great Hittite Empire: many ancient settlements, such as Mersin or Tarsus, are still thriving. There are hundreds of castles here, most dating back to the 9th to 13th centuries, when the area broke from the Byzantine Empire as the independent kingdom of Armenia. Beyond Cilicia, the Hatay is a finger of land pointing down to the Syrian border, annexed to Turkey in 1939. There is a greater sense of Asia here: the area has few foreign tourists. For those seeking the Turkish people, this is the place to come.

> *'Antioch is like the pantaloon whose clothes are far too wide for his lean shanks; the castle walls go climbing over rock and hill, enclosing an area from which the town has shrunk.'*
>
> GERTRUDE BELL,
> *The Desert and the Sown* (1907)

———•———

St Peter's Church, Antakya – official founding place of the Christian Church

Adada

Although virtually unknown to tourists, Adana is the fourth largest city in Turkey (after Istanbul, Ankara and Izmir), with a population of over 2 million. There has been a settlement here since the Hittite era, when it may have been Danunas, capital of King Asitawata, who also built Karatepe (► 20). Like all the surrounding cities, it has been a political football, overrun by a new invader almost every century, and in July 1998 it was the epicentre of a major earthquake.

Until the 20th century, Adana remained relatively insignificant, overshadowed by Tarsus and Antakya. Since the arrival of the railway, it has far outstripped its neighbours and is now the regional capital and a wealthy, vibrant university city, surrounded by heavy industry and fertile agricultural plains producing citrus, cotton and corn. Its only must-see sight is the New Mosque. All the other sights are within walking distance of it.

About 25km east of the city, İncirlik is a huge American airforce base with around 5,000 troops, and a village that has all the comforts of home, from McDonald's to Pizza Express! The nearest beach resort is at Karataş, 48km south.

What to See in Adana

ARKEOLOJİ MÜZESİ ⊕
(ARCHAEOLOGICAL MUSEUM)

There are some nice exhibits in this dreary museum, including classical and Hittite statuary, mosaics, bronzeware, jewellery, coins and early pottery, but it takes enthusiasm to get past the drab, poorly lit displays and general apathy.

MERKEZ CAMİ (NEW MOSQUE) ⊕⊕⊕

With a dome 51m high, space for 30,000 people and six minarets, this magnificent new mosque is a rivial in size to the Süleymaniye Camii in Istanbul. Outside, dome is elegantly heaped on dome, the shining white marble reflected in the river. The interior décor, using a mix of decorative tiles and Koranic calligraphy, liberally sprinkled with gold leaf, is based on Istanbul's Blue Mosque and promises to be every bit as spectacular. Construction of the mosque began in 1988, and there are further plans for a huge open plaza and museum of Islam.

From here, it is a pleasant walk along the Seyhan river to the 310m, multi-arched Taş Köprü (Stone Bridge), built by Emperor Hadrian (AD 117–138), and restored by Justinian, the Ottomans and various others (the last time was in 1950).

Sidebar (left column):

✚ 29F2
✉ 445km east of Alanya, on the N-400
ℹ Regional Directorate, Çınarlı Mah, Atatürk Caddesi 13 ☎ 0322-363 1287 (Head Office)
🍴 Choice of restaurants (££)
🚐 5km west of town: *dolmuş* to centre
🚉 North of centre, near top of Ziya Paşa Caddesi
↔ Karatepe (► 20), Mersin, Misis (► 84–5), Tarsus (► 90), Topprakale (► 91), Yılankalesi (► 92)

✉ Next to the Merkez Cami
🕐 Tue–Sun 8:30–12, 1–4:30. Closed Mon
♿ None
🖐 Cheap

✉ T Kemal Beriker Bulvari, next to the river
♿ None
🖐 Free
❓ Opening planned for 1999

Above: *selling* simit *(bread rings) by the old bridge, Adana*

MÜZESİ ETNOGRAFİCO (ETHNOGRAPHY MUSEUM) ⭐

Housed in a Byzantine church, this is a small but well-thought-out collection, with a variety of musical instruments, household objects, jewellery, carpets and *kilims*, traditional embroidery, illustrated manuscripts and a reconstruction nomads' tent.

✉ Özler Caddesi
🕐 Tue–Sun 8:30–12, 1:30–5:30. Closed Mon
♿ None
🎟 Cheap

ULU CAMİ (GREAT MOSQUE) ⭐⭐

A very different mosque, but equally beautiful, the Ulu Cami was built in 1541 as a legacy from Halil Bey, a member of the ruling Ramazanoğlu family, who died in 1507 and is buried here. The mosque's distinctively Syrian design has black and white marble stripes around the octagonal minaret, and black, white and yellow İznik tiles around the entrance and the *mihrab* (the niche showing the direction of Mecca).

Opposite is a still functioning *medrese* (religious school), built at the same time as the mosque. Near by are two other historic mosques: the Akça Mesçit and the Ramazanoğlu Camii, both built in the early 15th century, also in the Syrian style.

✉ To the left, off Abidin Paşa Caddesi, in the old town
🕐 Daily 8:30–5
♿ None
🎟 Free

The Merkez Cami is an impressive sight beyond the Taş Köprü

A Drive from Adana to Cappadocia

Distance
About 310km one way, from
Adana to Ürgüp

Time
Allow 3–4 hours one way. It is
possible to get a brief glimpse
in one long day. Preferably
allow 3 days

Start point
Adana
✛ 29F2

End point
Ürgüp
✛ 29E2

*Weird stone chimneys
turn the Cappadocia
landscape into a
fantasy world*

This can be only the most superficial introduction to
Cappadocia's weird landscape, which holds an immense
wealth of history and art. Cappadocia is a triangle of land
roughly bordered by Niğde, Nevşehir and Kayseri. Ten
million years ago, two volcanoes – Erciyes Dağ (3,916m)
and Hasan Dağ (3,268m) – spewed soft lava (tufa), ash and
mud over the local basalt plain. This has eroded unevenly,
creating extraordinary columns and cones (known as 'fairy
chimneys') in a dazzling array of colours, from purple to
yellow, russet and red. The tufa is soft until exposed to the
air, making it easy for generations, from the Hittites
onwards, to carve out at least 37 extraordinary underground cities, some housing up to 60,000 people. During
the early Christian years, the area became a refuge from
the Romans, and then from Arab invasions. The monks left
a stunning legacy of some 3,000 rock churches, many
vividly painted. Those with the time can explore the area by
horse, mountain bike or hot air balloon.

*Leave Adana on the E-90 or N-400,
heading west towards Tarsus (▶ 90).
After 35km, turn north on to the O-
21 motorway or the N-750. The
roads join after 64km, at Pozantı.
Continue for 46km, then take the N-
805 north to Niğde (53km).*

There are several fine Selçuk and Mongol
buildings and an 11th-century citadel in Niğde, but
the must-see sight is Eski Gümüş (14km north, off
the Kayseri road), a rock-cut monastery with superb
frescoes and an open courtyard. Kayseri makes
some of Turkey's finest carpets.

*After 10km, turn left on to the N-765.
After 17km, at Gölcük, turn left for the
Ilhara Valley.*

A path with 435 steps
drops down into
this 10km-long,
150m-deep gorge,
carved by the
Melendiz river. It
is an extraordinary
place, with an
estimated 4,500

man-made caves and 105 churches and shrines. Between them, narrow paths run through fabulous scenery rich in wildlife. Several of the churches along the valley are decorated with fine Byzantine frescoes and glory in descriptive names such as Direkli Kilise (Church with the Columns) and Kırk Damalı Kilise (Church with Forty Roofs).

Return to the main road and keep straight on for another 63km through Derinkuyu (17km) and Kaymaklı (9km) to Nevşehir.

The labyrinthine underground cities of Derinkuyu and Kaymaklı, created by carving tunnels between deep wells, are almost invisible from the surface. Linked by a 9km tunnel, they had constant temperature, humidity and good ventilation from air shafts. The upper storeys contained living quarters; the lower levels were for storage, fortifications, graveyards and dungeons. The top eight storeys (of a probable 20) are open at Derinkuyu; four at Kaymaklı.

Turn right along the N-767 for the Göreme Valley and Ürgüp (about 20km).

In the 6th–11th centuries, the Göreme valley, now a national park and open air museum, was Cappadocia's main centre of Christianity, with some magnificent Byzantine art. The tour takes in seven painted churches, culminating in the fabulous Tokalı Kilise (Buckle Church). Avanos, just north of Göreme, produces wonderful pottery. Ürgüp is an attractive town, with old Greek houses backing on to caves, and a thriving tourist centre with the region's main museum and numerous small hotels.

The glorious interior of the Tokalı Kilise

Lunch/accommodation
Ataman Hotel/Restaurant
✉ Orta Mah, Göreme (£££)
☎ 0384-271 2310

Tourist Offices
Regional Directorate
✉ Atatürk Bulv, Devlet Hastanesi Önü, Nevşehir
☎ 0384-213 3659/9604
✉ Kağnı Pazarı 01, Melihgazi, Kayseri
☎ 0352-222 3903
✉ Belediye Sarayı, C Blok, Kat: 3, Niğde ☎ 0388-232 3393
✉ Park İçi, Kayseri Caddesi, Ürgüp; next to the museum ☎ 0384 041 4059

✚ 29D1

✉ 128km east of Alanya;
223km west of Mersin on
the N-400

ℹ Otogar Binası Kat 2

☎ 0324-814 3529

🍴 Some restaurants (£)

♿ None

↔ Silifke (➤ 86–7)

Museum

✉ İskele Caddesi

☎ 0324-814 1677

🕐 Tue–Sun 8–5. Closed
Mon

💰 Cheap

*The battlements of
Mamure Kalesi guard the
southernmost point of the
Cilician coast*

ANAMUR ✪✪✪

Built on a small plain between the Sultansuys and Tatlısu rivers, surrounded by the Taurus mountains and cut off from both Alanya to the west and Mersin to the east by many kilometres of treacherous but spectacular roads along the sea cliffs, Anamur is a rarity. Although the town itself is a drab little place about 5km inland, its seaside twin, İskele, is a small, almost untouched seaside town whose few hotels are cheap. Most of the visitors are Turkish, but anyone willing to make the trek will find it very rewarding. Not only does it have one of Turkey's finest castles (Mamure Kalesi, ➤ 22), an excellent ancient city and a small but interesting **museum**; it also has a good beach. Local wildlife includes loggerhead turtles and a small colony of monk seals.

Occupying the southernmost tip of Anatolia, 6km east, Anamurium (meaning 'windy cape') was established by the Hittites in around 1200 BC, but first enters history with the invasion of the Assyrians in the 8th century BC. It became a bishopric in the early Byzantine era, but never really recovered from a devastating earthquake in AD 580, closely followed by the first Arab invasions. The impressive ruins remaining today mainly date from the 2nd to 5th centuries AD. Highlights include a necropolis as large and well-built as a town, some of its 350 tombs boasting painted interiors; a

The high walls of
Anamurium – overgrown
and largely unexcavated

bath and gymnasium; a basilica; a lighthouse; an odeon
and a theatre. The bath and several private houses still
have mosaic floors. There is a beach and picnic site at the
far end, under a cliff on which stand the last few remnants
of the citadel.

ANAVARZA (DİLEKKAYA)

The lower city at this remote, entirely unexcavated site
was almost entirely destroyed by an earthquake in Roman
times and was rebuilt by Emperor Justinian. It then
changed hands many times until it became a minor capital
of Armenia in 1100. It was abandoned in 1375. Visible
remains include a number of mosaics, a stadium, an
amphitheatre, a theatre, baths, a triumphal arch and
tombs. It takes some serious scrambling to climb up the
200m escarpment to the heavily defended citadel, built by
the Armenians on top of much older fortifications.

✚ 29F2
✉ 72km northeast of
Adana: left off N-400 at
Ceyhan; then right
towards Aysehoca
♿ None
 Free; use a local guide
↔ Karatepe (➤ 20), Misis
(➤ 85), Topprakale
(➤ 91), Yılankalesi
(➤ 92)

79

29F1

191km southeast of Adana, via the N-400/E-90 and N817/E-91

Choice of restaurants (£–£££)

Coaches from Adana and on to Syria; *dolmuş*

None

Çevlik, Harbiye (➤ 83), İskenderun (➤ 84), St Simeon's Monastery (➤ 90)

Sen Piyer Kilisesi

2km off Kurtuluş Caddesi, northeast of city centre

Tue–Sun 8–12, 1.30–6. Closed Mon. Citadel, open access

ANTAKYA

In the Hatay, as everywhere else in Turkey, there was a power vacuum after the death of Alexander the Great in 324 BC. Here, Seleukos Nikator I took control. In about 300 BC, he chose as his capital the small town of Antigonus, on the Orontes river, in the foothills of Mount Silpius. This not only barred the classic invasion route, but also stood right on the Silk Road that crossed from China through the Middle East to Europe. Renamed Antioch after Seleukos's father, the city prospered, especially after it was ceded to Rome in 64 BC. Within a century, it was the third largest city in the Roman Empire (after Rome and Alexandria), the capital of the Roman province of Syria, and was famous as a centre of religion, learning, science and, of course, trade. Amenities included aqueducts, street-lighting and a colonnaded main street 6.5km long, as well as the usual theatre, stadium, baths and other civic buildings. With a cosmopolitan population including a large Jewish community, it became one of the key centres of early Christianity.

Inevitably, life was not all easy. The Christians were ruthlessly persecuted. The city was nearly destroyed by two great fires, a massive outbreak of plague and several horrendous earthquakes, one of which was said to have killed 250,000 people. In 638, the city was conquered by the Muslim Persians. In 1084, it fell to the Selçuk Turks, and in 1098 it was besieged for nine months by the Crusaders, who set it up as a Christian principality. It was captured by the Mamelukes (Egyptian rulers) in 1268, became part of the Ottoman Empire in 1516 and, with the collapse of the Silk Road, decayed into a sleepy backwater. It was a French colony from 1918 until 1938, when the Turkish Army moved in; a year later it voted to join Turkey. Syria still lays claim to the area.

Modern Antakya is an attractive, friendly place, well off the beaten track. Tourism is small-scale, with very few Westerners; Arabic is the second language of the area. Yet there is undoubtedly still money in the city. The broad boulevards of the left bank contain some of the smartest shops in southern Turkey, in sharp contrast to the market stalls, kiosks and huddled old houses of the right bank old town. The central Hatay Müzesi (➤ 19) is a world-class museum of Roman mosaics.

St Peter lived in Antioch from AD 47 to 54, holding secret gatherings of converts in the 30m by 9m by 7m **Sen Piyer Kilisesi** (St Peter's Cave), just outside the city, and this is commonly regarded as the very first Christian church. It was here that Peter, Paul and Barnabas decided to call their religion 'Christian' (Acts 11:26), and it went on to become the seat of a powerful patriarch. The arched entrance built by the Crusaders in the 11th century was prettied up in 1863. Inside, the simple church has a plain stone altar, in front of which are some remnants of a 5th-

century AD mosaic floor. To the right is a spring, said to spout holy water; to the left an escape tunnel (now blocked). A winding 15km road leads on up to the ruined citadel, successively rebuilt from the 4th century BC to the 10th century AD.

St Peter's Church, a simple cave just outside ancient Antioch

A Walk Around Antakya

Distance
About 2km

Time
Allow 1–2 hours

Start point
Beside the Hatay Müzesi, on the city centre roundabout beside the Rana Köprüsü (bridge)
🚩 29F1
🚌 Dolmuş or taxi

End point
Rana Köprüsü
🚩 29F1
🚌 Dolmuş or taxi

Lunch
Anadolu (££)
✉ Hurriye Caddesi 50/C
☎ 0326-215 1541

Start at the Hatay Müzesi.

The Asi (Orontes) river neatly divides Antakya in two. To the left, the pleasant 'new' town owes a great deal to French inter-war town planning. Directly opposite the museum, on Atatürk Caddesi, are a splendidly ornate cinema and magnificent Ottoman mansion.

Cross the river on the Rana Köprüsü (Old Bridge).

The bridge looks ultra-modern, but lurking under the metal and tar is a 3rd-century AD stone bridge. Straight ahead, the imposing minaret of the Ulu Cami marks the start of the old town.

Turn half right along Hürriyet Caddesi, one of the main streets of the old town.

Restaurants, fast food joints and delectable sweet shops line this road, which curves up the hill, round some fine old houses, to a couple of elegant neo-classical mansions that form part of the university.

From here, continue uphill and turn left along Valiurgan Bulvari, or, more interestingly, go back down and wind your way through the maze of pretty back streets.

In either case, you will eventually come out on to Kurtuluş Caddesi, where rows of rundown mansions are festooned in doctors' boards.

Walk along Kurtuluş Caddesi until you reach the Habib Neccar Camii.

This mosque was built within the shell of a Byzantine church, with a 17th-century minaret.

Turn left down the hill on Kemal Paşa Caddesi. About halfway down, the covered side alleys fill with the stalls of the main bazaar. Choose your own route. You will inevitably end up back at the Rana Köprüsü.

The narrow, shady alleys at the heart of old Antakya are jammed with tiny shops and stalls

ÇEVLİK ⭐

Founded as his capital by the first Seleucid ruler, Seleukos Nikator I, in the 4th century BC, the ancient harbour of Seleucia ad Piera later served as Antioch's port. The tiny, modern village of Çevlik still has an attractive working harbour and a pleasant, if short stretch of beach. On the hill above, the Titus Tüneli is a massive, surprisingly impressive storm drain, carved from the rock by emperors Titus and Vespasian to protect the harbour from the effects of floods and silt. The water is not recommended for swimming due to pollution from nearby İskenderun (► 84). Samandağ, though billed as a resort, is a most unattractive place and best avoided.

✚	29F1
✉	Samandağ 25km west of Antakya; Çevlik 5km north of Samandağ
🍴	Several restaurants along the seafront in Çevlik (£)
🕐	Open access
♿	None
🎟	Titus Tüneli: cheap
↔	St Simeon's Monastery (► 90)

HARBİYE (DAPHNE) ⭐

Ancient Daphne was a busy place. The nymph Daphne, hotly pursued by Apollo, prayed for delivery and was turned into a laurel bush. Apollo took a branch and wove himself a laurel wreath, which became the symbol of victory. It was also here that Cyparissus accidently shot his pet stag. Apollo turned the grieving man into a cypress tree, which became the symbol of mourning. Most contentiously, it was here that Paris was asked to judge a goddesses' beauty competition. He awarded the golden apple to Aphrodite, who promised him in return the loveliest woman in the world, Helen – who happened to be married to someone else. And that led to the Trojan War.

Daphne (now called Harbiye) was the summer resort of Roman Antioch, a wealthy suburb whose 2nd to 4th-century villas revealed a treasure trove of mosaics (► 19). Anthony and Cleopatra were married here in 40 BC. Today, the deep, green valley and a waterfall are overwhelmed by houses and tatty souvenir and snack stalls.

✚	29F1
✉	8km south of Antakya on the N-825
♿	None
🎟	Free
↔	Antakya (► 19 and 80–2), Çevlik (► 83), St Simeon's Monastery (► 90)

The richly adorned walls of the mosaics museum in Antakya

29F2

56km north of Antakya, on the N-825

Atatürk Bulv 49/B

0326-614 1620

Antakya (➤ 80–2)

Above: *romantic and tragic, the Kiz Kalesi stands marooned on an islet 200m off-shore*

29E1

25km east of Silifke

Daily 8:30–5

Several restaurants and cafés along the seafront overlooking Kiz Kalesi (££)

Dolmuş to Korykos; ask one of the boatmen at the beach motel next door to take you out to the island

None

Free, except for the boat

Narlıkuyu (➤ 86), Silifke (➤ 86–7), Uzuncaburç (➤ 92)

29E2

72km west of Adana on the N-400

Several restaurants in harbour area (££)

İsmet İnönü Bulv 5

0324-238 3270/1

İSKENDERUN

This busy commercial and industrial city was founded in 333 BC by Alexander the Great, following his decisive victory against the Persians in the Battle of Issos. For centuries, it lost out as a port to nearby Seleuceia ad Piera (Çevlik, ➤ 83), but came into its own with the industrial revolution and is now a belching hellhole of pollution. To the south, the town of Belen (now a popular suburb above the smog) lies on a mountain pass known as the Gates of Syria, the main route into Turkey for the camel caravans of the Silk Road and successive invading armies.

KARATEPE (➤ 20, TOP TEN)

KIZ KALESI

Two castles stare at each other across 200m of sea. Off-shore, perched on a tiny island only accessible by boat, is Kız Kalesi (Maiden's Castle), built in 1104 by Byzantine admiral Eugenius during the early days of the Crusades. Its name derives from a local legend that a king, on hearing from an oracle that his beloved daughter would die of a snake bite, shut her up on the snake-free island. Unfortunately, a viper hid in a basket of fruit taken into the castle, and the prophecy was fulfilled.

On shore, 13th-century Korykos Castle reuses the materials of a Roman fortification, part of a large and flourishing ancient city, mentioned by Herodotos in the 5th century BC, of which various other remains are scattered across the headland. About 8km north, at Adam Kayalar, 1st–2nd-century AD Roman relief sculptures are cut into the cliff face.

MERSİN (İÇEL)

Until the mid-19th century, Mersin, situated on the fertile Cilician Plain, was a rather scruffy hamlet with a few fishermen's huts. Today it is a city with a population of over 600,000, which tries to be a tourist destination but is really an industrial town. The centre is attractively laid out, with broad boulevards and shady gardens along the

seafront, and there is an interesting little **museum**.

Mersin has one of the longest histories in Turkey. About 9km south, in a scruffy park in suburban Soğuksu, the extraordinary tumulus of Yümüktepe has revealed 23 layers of civilisations, dating from 6300 BC to the 12th century AD. There is little to see here now; finds are on display in the museum.

Soloi, 14km west at Viranşehir, was a trading city founded by colonists from Rhodes in the 7th century BC. In about 64 BC, Pompey changed the city's name to Pompeiopolis in honour of his victory over the local pirates. The city was destroyed by an earthquake in the late Byzantine period.

MİSİS (YAKAPINAR) ✪✪

This is a very unusual site. There is an ancient city, said to have been founded by Hittite King Mopsus, curled around the gardens and side streets of the village. However, Misis is probably even more interesting for the slice of Turkish rural life it provides. The men play backgammon in the street; the children herd goats, and the women toil making bread for dinner. The much-heralded museum is simply one large Roman mosaic, said to represent Noah's Ark, covered and left *in situ*. Walk around the village and you will also discover a Roman stone bridge, still very much in use, remnants of the city walls, an aqueduct, a temple, a theatre, an even more ancient tell (mound), an Ottoman caravansaray and a couple of mosques.

Museum
- ✉ Atatürk C Kültür Merkezi yanı
- ☎ 0324-231 9618
- 🕐 Mon–Sat 8–4:30. Closed Sun
- ♿ None
- 🎫 Cheap

- ✚ 29F2
- ✉ About 40km east of Adana, 3km off the N-400
- 🕐 Museum officially open daily 8:30–12, 1–4:30; in practice kept locked: local children will let you in
- 🍴 A couple of simple cafés in the village (£)
- ♿ None
- 🎫 Museum: cheap
- ↔ Adana (➤ 74–5), Topprakale (➤ 91), Yılankalesi (➤ 92)

Plastic is big in Turkey

NARLIKUYU ⊙

🔲 29E1

✉ 20km east of Silifke; the caves are 3km inland, both off the N-400

🕐 Daily 8:30–5

🍴 Several good fish restaurants line the waterfront (££); café next to the caves' car park (£)

🚌 Dolmuş

♿ None

👜 Cheap

The coastal village of Narlıkuyu ('well of the pomegranate') was once a port with a famous bath complex, of which only the 4th-century AD floor mosaic, depicting the Three Graces, remains. Water from the spring that fed the complex (still bubbling today) was said to give wisdom to those who drank from it.

A short distance inland are the Corycian Caves, better known as Cennet ve Cehennem (Heaven and Hell), and regarded as sacred by pagans, Christians and Muslims alike. At the edge of the Cave of Heaven stands the temple of Zeus Corychios, which was used as the

foundation of a 4th to 5th-century Christian basilica (now next to the car park). To reach Heaven (Cennet Deresi), climb down 452 steps to the bottom of the larger chasm (200m long, 90m wide and 70m deep), where a small Byzantine chapel dedicated to the Virgin blocks the entrance of the Cave-Gorge of Hell. Continue along a slippery path down the gorge for 200m, listening out for the intermittent roar of an underground river (thought by some to have been the Styx), to the cave entrance to Hades, the site of an oracle.

Above: the Three Graces still decorate the long-abandoned bath-house at Narlıkuyu

Right: Silifke's massive fortress totally dominated the surrounding plains

About 75m north is a 120m-deep, 50sq-m pit – the Cehennem (the pit of Hell), where Zeus imprisoned Typhon, the many-headed, fire-breathing serpent, who was father of Cerberus, guard dog of Hell. This can be reached only by experienced climbers.

Under the souvenir shop is a 20m-deep, 200m-long cave system with beautiful stalactites and stalagmites, which is said to be beneficial to asthma sufferers. There are still some remains of a Byzantine town in the surrounding countryside.

SİLİFKE ⊙⊙

🔲 29D1

✉ 217km east of Anamur; 161km west of Adana on the N-400

ℹ Gazi Mah, Veli Gürten Bozbey Cad 6
   ☎ 0324-714 1151

↔ Kiz Kalesi (➤ 84), Narlıkuyu (➤ 86), Uzuncaburç (➤ 92)

This small, busy market town, about 10km inland, surrounded by fertile agricultural plains, was one of nine founded by and named after Alexander's egocentric general, Seleukos Nikator I, in the 3rd century BC. It stands on the Göksu Nehri (Sky Blue Water), in which Frederick Barbarossa drowned in 1190 (➤ 88). It is dominated by a magnificent **castle**, built by the Byzantines but heavily altered by the Armenians and Crusaders before reverting to Turkish hands in the late 13th century.

From the battlements there is a splendid view over the whole town, which helps pinpoint the remains of ancient Seleukeia Tracheia. On the river is a modern, multi arched stone bridge, still sporting Vespasian's inscription of AD 78. Near by, a park surrounds the ancient acropolis first fortified by the Assyrians in the 8th century BC: there are faint traces of a Roman theatre and the Seleucid fort. The town was home to the famous Roman oracle of Apollo Sarpedonios, whose temple is on İnönü Bulvari. Other fragments include a stretch of aqueduct, a massive Byzantine water cistern, and the necropolis, all near the foot of the castle hill. The various finds are collected in the town **museum**.

About 1km west is the tiny 4th-century AD Byzantine cave church of Haghia Thekla, the hermitage of a 1st-century AD saint, St Paul's first convert, who is said to have flown bodily up to heaven to escape martyrdom.

Castle

✉ 4km from the town centre, turn off the main road at the western (Anamur) entrance to the town

🕐 Daily 8:30–5

🍴 Restaurant/café beside the car park (£)

♿ None

💷 Cheap

Museum

✉ Taşucu Yolu Üzeri (main Antalya road)

☎ 0324-714 1019

🕐 Tue–Sun 8–5

💷 Cheap

Mevlâna Tekke is a place of pilgrimage and the heart of the dervish monastic order

A Drive to Konya

This is one of the most beautiful roads in Turkey. The first half follows a winding mountain route; the second is a flat, straight drive across the plains.

Head north from Silifke on the N-715.

About 7km north of Silifke on the N-715, a memorial marks the spot where the Holy Roman Emperor, Frederick Barbarossa, drowned in 1190, in the Göksu River, while leading the Third Crusade. He was pickled in vinegar to preserve him for burial at St Peter's Cathedral, Antioch (➤ 80) before being returned to Germany.

Continue along the main road for 76km to Mut.

The busy market town of Mut has a 14th-century mosque, Lal Ağı Camii, a fortress and two domed tombs. About 20km north, the well-preserved Byzantine monastery of Alahan (2km off the main road) overlooks the wild Göksu Gorge.

Return to the main road and head north for 73km to Karaman.

Distance
252km

Time
Allow 2–3 days for the round-trip, including sightseeing and side tracks. This excursion can be done in conjunction with the Cappadocia tour (➤ 76–7) by taking the N-300 via Aksaray to Nevşehir (207km).

Start/end point
Silifke
✚ 29D1

Lunch
Restaurants in Mut, Karaman, roadside cafés along the route; the best option is to take a picnic up to Binbir Kilise

Dinner
Horozlu Han Kervansaray (£££)
Restored medieval caravansaray, with floor shows on many evenings.
✉ Konya-Ankara Yolu Üzeri, TNP Yani, Konya
☎ 0332-248 3115

Between 1277 and 1467, Karaman became the centre of a powerful autonomous emirate. Several monuments date to the period, including the fortress, the mosque, Yunus Emre Camii, and several religious houses and schools – the Hatuniye Medresesi, the İbrahim Bey İmareti and the Ak Tekke. The small museum holds fascinating finds from the 6th-millennium BC site of Canhasan, about 13km northeast. The valley of Binbir Kilesi (1,001 churches) is 38km north of town, near the village of Dinek (the last 8km are up a rough but passable track). From the 5th–6th and 9th–14th centuries it was crammed with monasteries, many of which, including some with frescoes, survive in scattered ruins.

About 72km north of Karaman, Çatalhöyük (around 6500–5400 BC) is the second oldest known city in the world (after Jericho), the first place known to use irrigation, keep domestic animals and make carpets. There is little to see here now: the finds are all in Ankara's Museum of Anatolian Civilisations.

Continue for a further 56km to Konya.

Konya is a large, rapidly growing, noisy and chaotic city. It was the Selçuk capital from 1071 to 1308 and probably still has a good claim to be the Islamic capital of Turkey; be aware of religious sensibilities. By far the most important sight in town is the **Mevlâna Tekke Müzesi.** This was the monastery of the 13th-century mystic philosopher and poet, Jalal ad-Din ar-Rumi, better known as Mevlâna, founder of the Sufi monastic order of dervishes, who worshipped God through music and dance. The building has been a museum since Atatürk abolished the order in 1925, but it is still a centre of pilgrimage, containing Mevlâna's tomb and, supposedly, hairs from the Prophet Mohammed's beard, along with a magnificent collection of art, ancient manuscripts and rare 13th-century *kilims.* Other museums in the city include the magnificent Selçuk Karatay Medresesi, containing a wonderful collection of ceramics; the İnce Minare Medresesi, used as a lapidary and wood-carving museum, and an archaeological museum. There are also several beautiful mosques and religious institutions, of which the finest must be the 13th-century Selçuk Alâeddin Camii.

Return to Silifke along the same route.

Accommodation
Otel Selçuk (££)
✉ Alâeddin Caddesi 4, Konya
☎ 0332-350 4290; fax: 0332-353 2529

Tourist Information
✉ Mevlâna Cad 21, Konya
☎ 0332-351 1074
❓ Festival of the Dancing Dervishes, 9–17 Dec. This annual pilgrimage shows the 'whirling dervishes' at their finest. Booking essential

Mevlâna Tekke Müzesi
✉ Mevlâna Meydanı
☎ 0332-331 1215
🕐 Summer: Mon 10–6, Tue–Sun 9–6; winter: Tue–Sun 9–5:30
✋ Moderate

The drive north to Konya is a magnificent scenic treat; give yourself time to savour the surroundings

⊠ Turn off the Samandağ road 22km west of Antakya
⊙ Open access
♿ None
💷 Free
❓ Çevlik (➤ 83), Antakya (➤ 80–2)

Below: *Cleopatra's Gate, the entrance to ancient Tarsus*

✚ 29E2
⊠ 38km west of Adana
🍴 Choice of cafés and restaurants (£–££)
♿ None
↔ Adana (➤ 74), Mersin (➤ 84)

Museum
⊠ Kulat Paşa Medrese, Tahakhane Mah, 155 Sok, No 1
☎ 0324-613 0625
⊙ Tue–Sun, 8–5. Closed Mon
♿ None
💷 Moderate

ST SIMEON'S MONASTERY

One of the oddest of the early Christian zealots was St Simeon Stylites the Younger, who sat on a pillar to commune with God. Starting on a humble rock, he eventually graduated to a 13m column of stone on a high promontory overlooking the sea. There he remained for 25 years, chained to the pillar. A large monastery grew up around the column to cater for the many pilgrims who came to listen to his pronouncements; and he started a trend, with some 250 people eventually inhabiting columns across Syria. Today, the base of the column remains, surrounded by the ruined monastery. The views are magnificent.

TARSUS

Legend says Tarsus was founded by Seth, son of Adam; archaeologists say the town has been here since about 3000 BC. It remained the most important city in the area until its lagoon silted up and cut it off from the sea. In 333 BC Alexander the Great caught a chill swimming in the waterfall; in 41 BC, Mark Anthony summoned Cleopatra here for punishment after she backed the wrong side in the Battle of Philippi. She arrived in glory and he fell in love. A few decades later, a local Jew named Saul became St Paul (➤ 14). Over the years Tarsus has been sacked by the Arabs, Selçuks, Crusaders, Armenians, Mamelukes and Ottomans. Little remains of its illustrious past, but the crumbling Ottoman houses and narrow streets of the old town still groan with age.

At the city entrance is a Roman arch, known as the Kancık Kapışı (Gate of the Bitch) or Cleopatra's Gate, although it has nothing to do with her. A few blocks away are two mosques: the Kilise Cami which is a converted 14th-century Armenian church; and the Makam Camii, said to mark the burial place of the Prophet Daniel. Near by there is a religious school, the Kulat Paşa Medrese (built in 1570), which houses a small **museum**, with classical and Hittite exhibits, manuscript displays and jewellery.

The old town surrounds

Left: *artefacts from a past age on display at Tarsus Museum*

a covered market and open square in which a Roman road is being excavated. Near by, St Paul's Well, with supposedly curative water, is theoretically St Paul's boyhood home. On the edge of town, the Şelale is a delightfully cool waterfall.

TOPPRAKALE
😊😊

The swirl of modern roads around this formidable fortress emphasises its strategic importance at the gateway between Syria and Turkey. Built of forbiddingly dark volcanic rock by Byzantine Emperor Nicophorus II Pocas (963–9), it changed hands numerous times, including a short spell when it was occupied by the crusading Knights of St John, who redesigned and modelled it on the impregnable Krak des Chevaliers castle in Syria. It was eventually abandoned in 1337.

➕ 29F2
📧 75km east of Adana, at the crossroads of the N-400/E-5 and N-817/E-91
🕐 Daily 8:30–5
♿ None
🖐 Officially free; guide recommended
↔ Karatepe (► 20), Misis (► 85), Yılankalesi (► 92)

> ### *Did you know ?*
>
> *Born in 356 BC, Alexander was the eldest son of Philip II of Macedon. Bent on restoring Greece to former glories, his first action on succeeding to the throne was to gather an army and march east to liberate Asia Minor from the Persian king Darius the Great. Over the next nine years he amassed a great empire, but died of a fever in Babylon at the age of 32.*

UZUNCABURÇ (OLBA/DIOCAESARIA)

Now a remote upland village, whose name means 'high tower', after its imposing 22.5m, five-storey Hellenistic tower (late 3rd century BC), this settlement has been here since Hittite days. In about 295 BC, Seleucid ruler Seleukos Nikator (321–280 BC) built a temple to Zeus, the earliest in Asia Minor to use a colonnade; several Corinthian columns still stand. Over the next century its priests gained power as a dynasty of priest-kings, the Teukrides, who established the town of Olba around the temple. They continued to rule under Roman control, although the town changed its name during Vespasian's reign (AD 69–79) to Diocaesarea. The ruins, scattered around and to the north of the village include a Hellenistic pyramid tomb, Roman colonnaded street and monumental arch, a 2nd-century AD theatre, a nymphaeum (fountain) connected to a water supply network still used today, a temple of Tyche and the necropolis.

If you're thirsty, try one of the area's specialities, *kenger kahve* (coffee made from acanthus) or *pekmez* (boiled, concentrated grape juice). Local handicrafts include rugs, leather bags, embroidery and *meşe külü* soap, made from oak ash.

YILANKALESİ (SNAKE CASTLE)

This splendid medieval castle, all bastions and battlements, with well-preserved dungeons and living quarters, is one of many built to defend the plains east of Adana in the 13th century, possibly by Leo III (1270–89), while he was crown prince and the area was a breakaway Armenian state. Its name comes from a local legend that it was the lair of an evil half-man, half-snake, eventually killed in Tarsus while attempting to kidnap the king's daughter.

UZUNCABURÇ (OLBA/DIOCAESARIA)

- 29E2
- 30km north of Silifke
- Open access
- Simple café in the village (£)
- *Dolmuş* from tourist office or Atatürk Square, Silifke
- None
- Moderate (if caretaker is present)
- Silifke (► 86)

YILANKALESİ (SNAKE CASTLE)

- 29F2
- 48km east of Adana, 3km south of the N-400
- Officially daily 8:30–5, unofficially open access
- Café/restaurant in the car park (£)
- *Dolmuş* to the turn off the N-400
- None
- Cheap
- Karatepe (► 20), Misis (► 85), Topprakale (► 91)
- Gruelling climb over rocks from car park to walls

A temple fit for kings – the Corinthian colonnade at the temple of Zeus, Uzuncaburç

Where To...

Above: *a banana stall on the roadside, Anamur*
Right: *the traditional sounds of the Antalya musician*

Lycia

Prices
There is relatively little difference in price between the various restaurants in Turkey. The difference comes in what you eat. The following breakdown is based on the cost of an average two-course meal (eg *meze*, *kebab*, salad and bread) with non-alcoholic drinks. Expect to pay considerably more for fish. The tumbling value of the lira will also affect the price.

£	= 1–1.5 million lira (US$4–6)
££	= 1.5–3 million lira (US$6–12)
£££	= 3 million lira upwards (US$12–20)

One of the greatest delights of a holiday in Turkey is the food, which is excellent, extremely healthy (➤ 50–1), and can be sampled during leisurely afternoons and evenings at a table on an outdoor terrace in a shady garden overlooking the sea.

Demre (Kale)
Güneyhan Restaurant (£)
Simple but pleasant restaurant, with outdoor terrace, well placed beside St Nicholas's Church.

✉ **Saint Nicolas Kilisesi Yani** ☎ **0242-871 3810**

İpek Restoran (£)
Simple but delicious, this is a cheap, cheerful eatery with a good local reputation.

✉ **Gökyazi Mah** ☎ **0242-871 5448** 🕐 **All year, lunch and dinner**

Fethiye
Anfora (££)
One of the smarter-looking restaurants in Fethiye, with jazz photographs and giant pot plants. Turkish and continental food. Usually reasonably quiet, but with occasional invasions by tour groups.

✉ **Paspatur Hamam Sokak 5** 🕐 **Lunch and dinner**

Güneş (££)
Well-established restaurant in the bazaar area, with tables indoors and out. Hot and cold starters, meat and fish. No surprises.

✉ **Likya Sokak 4–5** ☎ **0252-614 2276** 🕐 **Lunch and dinner**

Meğri (££)
A long-running favourite with a large terrace and excellent seafood, *meze* and grills.

✉ **Ordukan Aş, Eski Cami Geçidi, Likya Sokak 8–9**

☎ **0252-614 4046** 🕐 **Summer only**

Ratef Restaurant (££)
A long-lived and attractive fish restaurant, Ratef occupies one of the best sites in Fethiye, on the promenade, beside the fishing harbour. An ideal place to while away warm summer evenings.

✉ **Kordon Boyu** ☎ **0252-614 1106** 🕐 **All year**

Uysallar (££)
One of the best of many restaurants crowded into the narrow streets of this vibrant old town area. The food is good, the atmosphere great.

✉ **Hamam Sokak Paspatur Mevkii 14** ☎ **0252-614 6524** 🕐 **Summer only**

Finike
Deniz 2 (£)
You may never see a menu in this simple, local restaurant on the main road, fronted by tables in cheerful red and white gingham. The owner will suggest a suitable meal from what is available that day – the result is excellent.

✉ **Kordon Caddesi** ☎ **0242-855 2282** 🕐 **All year, daily, lunch and dinner**

Petek (££)
This pretty restaurant on the main road, overlooking the harbour, has friendly service and does an excellent fish platter, as well as grills and more adventurous dishes.

✉ **Mahmut Nedim Kunt** ☎ **0242-855 1782** 🕐 **Open, but unheated, in winter; lunch and dinner daily**

Kalkan
Alternatif (££)
Popular British-run restaurant

that collects the best recipes from across the world, with daily specials from China, Mexico, France or the Pacific. Dinner is leisurely, and vegetarians and other special diets can be catered for with warning. Book ahead.

✉ **Yaliboyu Mah** ☎ **0242-844 3571** 🕐 **Summer only, lunch and dinner**

Belgin's Kitchen (££)
The best of Turkish cookery, with mouthwatering *börek*, *köfte* and *mantı*, served Ottoman-style; diners recline on piles of cushions on carpet-clad floors.

✉ **Yaliboyu Mah** ☎ **0242-844 3614** 🕐 **Summer only, lunch and dinner**

Doy-Doy (£)
Simple, straightforward Turkish food in a shady garden overlooking the harbour.

✉ **Yaliboyu Mah** ☎ **0242-844 3114** 🕐 **Summer only, lunch and dinner**

Korsan (£)
A pleasant, harbour-front restaurant serving excellent kebabs, salads and seafood.

✉ **Yaliboyu Mah** ☎ **0242-844 3622** 🕐 **Summer only, lunch and dinner**

Kaş

Chez Evy (££)
Charming, small, back-street restaurant, artfully fusing the best of French country cooking and Turkish style. It's very popular, so book ahead.

✉ **Terzi Sokak 4** ☎ **0242-836 1253** 🕐 **Summer only**

Eriş (££)
Long-established restaurant in an old Ottoman house, just off the seafront. No views, but the ambience is attractive, the service friendly and the food good, with a range of more complex Turkish dishes to offset the simple grills and fish.

✉ **Uzun Çarşi Caddesi, Orta Sokak 13** ☎ **0242-836 1057** 🕐 **All year, lunch and dinner**

Mercan (££)
Slick, popular restaurant with a large, outdoor terrace in the best position in town – right on the harbour front. The food – seafood and Turkish grills and kebabs – is good, but the prices are hiked by location.

✉ **Yat Limanı** ☎ **0242-836 1209** 🕐 **All year, lunch and dinner**

Oba Ev Yemekleri (£)
Mum cooks, her sons wait tables and the daughter ladles out huge portions of beef stew and lentil soup in this delightfully informal family restaurant away from the seafront. The traditional Turkish stews make a welcome change from kebabs and salad, and there is a shady garden terrace behind.

✉ **Çukurbağli Caddesi** ☎ **0242-836 1687** 🕐 **All year, lunch and dinner**

Smiley's (££)
Just behind the harbour front, this small, homely restaurant does a broad range of Turkish and international food, and has an attractive bar with a fireplace (great in winter) and a variety of secondhand books, including some in English.

✉ **Uzun Çarşi, Orta Sokak 11** ☎ **0242-836 2812** 🕐 **All year, lunch and dinner**

What's What
There are several categories of restaurant, starting with the all-encompassing *restoran*. A *lokanta* is a cafeteria serving a variety of stews, kept warm in a bain-marie. A *çorbacı* specialises in soup, a *kebapcı* or *köfteci* in kebabs (such as the *döner* kebab stalls on every street corner). A *meyhane* is a bar with added food (usually extremely uncomfortable for women).

Meals

Breakfast (*kahvaltı*) is served 7:30–10AM and consists of bread, cheese, olives, tomatoes and honey, with tea or coffee. Frills range from fruit juice and boiled eggs to yoghurt, fruit salad and patisseries. Lunch (*öğle yemeği*, 12:30–2:30) and dinner (*akşam yemeği*, 7–10PM) are both usually sit-down hot meals; for typical courses, ➤ 50–1.

Kemer

Akdeniz (£)

Built like a scout hut, with a basketball court beside it, this barn of a restaurant on the seafront looks grim in winter but comes into its own in season, when the outdoor terrace is lit and the weather is balmy. The food is standard Turkish grills and seafood.

✉ Deniz Caddesi 7 ☎ 0242-814 1219 🕐 All year, lunch and dinner

Derya Türk Mutfaği (£)

Unpretentious, friendly little local café near the tourist information office, serving excellent food. Less appetising specialities include lamb's brain and tripe soups, alongside more usual kebabs and *meze*.

✉ Liman Caddesi, Kemer ☎ 0242-814 4775 🕐 All year, lunch and dinner

Kemer Marina (££)

One of the more upmarket restaurants in town, serving the marina on which it stands, but always ready to welcome refugees from all-inclusive catering. The cuisine is Turkish, the food is good and there is a small bar.

✉ Yat Limanı (on the edge of the marina) ☎ 0242-814 1192

Marmaris

Alba (££–£££)

Exclusive hilltop restaurant with fine views and delicious European cuisine.

✉ Kaleiçi 30, Sokak 10 ☎ 0252-412 4299 🕐 Lunch and dinner

Antique (££–£££)

This first-floor balcony restaurant overlooking the Netsel Marina provides delightful views and cool breezes on hot summer nights. The food is delicious, with excellent salads. There is a café/bar for light snacks.

✉ Netsel Marina ☎ 0252-412 2708

Dede (££)

Thoroughly touristy place at the tourist office end of a long line of seafront restaurants. The huge menu, in English, German and Russian, boils down to the usual Turkish selection of chicken, fish and kebabs. Indoor and outdoor tables.

✉ Barbaros Caddesi 15 ☎ 0252-413 1289 🕐 8AM–midnight

Drunken Crab (£)

Small fish restaurant with few pretentions, no frills and good, simple food.

✉ Bar Street ☎ 0252-412 3970 🕐 Lunch and dinner

Mr Zek (££)

A popular, sociable and relaxing restaurant with light, live background music. The food is good, with some decent soups, fish and meat main courses and a broad selection of European and Turkish desserts.

✉ Yat Limanı (near tourist office) ☎ 0252-413 4123 🕐 Lunch and dinner

Mona Titti (££)

The brightly coloured exterior is easy to spot on the waterfront between the marina and the mermaid statue. The menu is quite imaginative and the curries are some of the best you are likely to enjoy on the coast. Reservations are sometimes necessary.

✉ Atatürk Caddesi, Marmaris

☎ 0252-412 8799 🕓 Lunch and dinner

Pineapple (££)
Residents rate this ground-floor restaurant in the Netsel Marina as one of the top half-dozen in Marmaris. The international menu may include anything from French onion soup to Thai curry.
✉ **Netsel Marina** ☎ **0252-412 0976** 🕓 **8AM–late**

Rovers Return (£)
The food – sausage and chips etc – will be familiar to addicts of the long-running English soap opera which gives this restaurant its name, the setting – a pleasant seaside garden – is a distinct improvement. It also has a cocktail bar.
✉ **Behind the Atlas Hotel, Kemel El, Marmaris** 🕓 **8AM–9PM**

Ölüdeniz
Beyaz Yunus (££)
Sea views, wicker chairs, cool surroundings and imaginative Turkish and international food.
✉ **Belcekiz, near Padirali** ☎ **0252-616 6036** 🕓 **Summer only, lunch and dinner**

Restaurant La Turquoise (££)
Poolside restaurant, with live Turkish music. The ambience is fine and the attempt at French cuisine valiant.
✉ **Montana Pine Resort** ☎ **0252-616 6366** 🕓 **Lunch and dinner**

Olympos
Park Restaurant (££)
Wonderful country restaurant in a converted mill, with a shady terrace, trout so fresh it's still swimming, seafood stews and traditional Turkish dishes.
✉ **Ulupınar Köyü, Ulupınar (near the turning off the main road, 30km west of Kemer)** ☎ **0242-825 7213** 🕓 **Summer only, lunch and dinner**

Ulupınar Prima Restaurant (££)
Comfortable, welcoming country restaurant on the main road near the Olympos turning, serving local specialities, including trout and herb salads.
✉ **Ulupınar (30km west of Kemer)** 🕓 **Summer only, lunch and dinner**

Patara
Golden Restaurant (£)
Popular, basic Turkish restaurant in the centre of the village, attached to one of the best local *pansiyons*. Trout normally features on the menu beside the kebabs.
✉ **Gelemiş Köyü** ☎ **0242-843 5162** 🕓 **Summer only, lunch and dinner**

Saklıkent
Hüseyin Güseli'in Yeri (£)
Family-run restaurant offering Turkish pancakes and grills, all cooked over a wood fire.
✉ **On the approach road to Saklıkent Gorge** ☎ **0252-636 8113** 🕓 **Summer only, lunch and dinner**

Yaka Park (££)
A restored windmill stands at the centre of this wonderful park, trout farm and restaurant, with the fish wriggling through fresh-water canals between the tables and along the bar.
✉ **Yaka Köyü** ☎ **0252-638 2011** 🕓 **Summer only, lunch and dinner**

Offal Truth
The Turks believe in using every part of the animal, and lambs' offal is frequently on the menu. Liver is particularly common, and is even turned into burgers. Two of the most common dishes which the squeamish might want to avoid are Beyin Salatası, a salad of sliced, marinaded brains, and İşkembe Corbası, tripe soup which tastes like warm lard with added flour.

Pamphylia, Cilicia & the Hatay

Noah's Feast

After Noah had sailed for 40 days and 40 nights, the flood waters finally began to subside. To celebrate, Mrs Noah put together a grand feast containing all 40 ingredients left on the Ark. The resulting dessert, Aşure, is a sort of sweet stew of pulses, fruit and nuts. It is still served as a celebratory dish throughout Turkey, associated particularly with the end of the 10-day fast on the 10th day of the Islamic month of Muharram. The ready-mix supermarket version is inferior, averaging only 20 ingredients.

Pamphylia

Alanya

Arzum Mantı Evi (£)

Plain, honest, cheap home cooking, specialising in *mantı* (Turkish ravioli). Vegetarian options available.

✉ **Atatürk Caddesi** ☎ **0242-513 9393**

Bistro Bellman (£–££)

Huge harbour-front restaurant, whose Swedish-Turkish owner serves pork and Scandinavian cuisine along with Turkish options.

✉ **Harbourfront** ☎ **0242-512 1992** 🕐 **All year, lunch and dinner**

Garden Restaurant (££)

Away from the seafront and most other tourists, this is a quiet, atmospheric restaurant with good food, live guitar music or jazz in the evenings, and an open fire in winter.

✉ **Keykubat Caddesi 5** ☎ **0242-513 8561** 🕐 **All year, daily lunch and dinner**

İskele Bar and Restaurant (££)

Popular local hangout with excellent sea food, *meze*, grills and a variety of international staples, live music and harbour views.

✉ **İskele Caddesi** ☎ **0242-513 1822** 🕐 **All year, lunch and dinner**

Odeon (££)

Calm, secluded garden restaurant, tucked away from the street behind an old Ottoman mansion. The Turkish-German owners provide excellent Turkish food with a little continental polish.

✉ **Damlataş Caddesi 32** ☎ **0242-513 1354**

Yakamoz (£££)

Attractive, busy fish restaurant and café, with excellent food and fine views over the harbour.

✉ **İskele Caddesi 39** ☎ **0242-512 2303** 🕐 **All year, lunch and dinner**

Alarahani

Alarahan (£)

Following a millennium of tradition, this restaurant, right beside the ancient caravansaray, offers a full range of meals (including breakfast), a pretty terrace overlooking the river, a souvenir shop and, for the more active, whitewater rafting.

✉ **Alarahan Yanı, Çakallar Köyü, Alarahan** ☎ **0242-547 8252** 🕐 **All year, breakfast, lunch and dinner**

Antalya

A La Turca's (£££)

This restaurant has its own garden and serves excellent sea bass, but prices soon mount up.

✉ **Uzun Çarsi Sokak 48** ☎ **0242-243 1903**

Develi Restaurant (££)

Pleasant surroundings in the Konyaaltı beach front area, and traditional Turkish cuisine, including several specialities from the southeast.

✉ **Konyaaltı, Birinci Arap Suyu** ☎ **0242-329 1200** 🕐 **Daily, lunch and dinner**

Hisar Turiskik Tesisi (£££)

The quality of the food does not always match up to the incomparable setting, but a stop here is worth it for the wonderful atmosphere, with a restaurant, bar and coffee corner set in the arched rooms of the fortress walls overlooking the old harbour.

✉ **Cumhuriyet Meydanı, Tophanealtı** ☎ 0242-241 5281 ⏰ Daily, lunch and dinner

Kral Sofrası (King's Table) (££)

Old-established local favourite, serving excellent Turkish and international food on a terrace overlooking the old harbour. Advance booking recommended.

✉ **Old Harbour, Kaleiçi** ☎ 0242-241 2198 ⏰ Daily, lunch and dinner

La Trattoria (£££)

An Italian *trattoria* straight off the streets of London, courtesy of the Turkish-English owners. Here, novelty has made it one of the trendiest places in town. The décor is pleasing, the service friendly and efficent and the food, including sticky puddings, delicious. Not a kebab in sight.

✉ **Fevzi Çakmak Caddesi 3/C (opposite the Belediye)** ☎ 0242-243 3931 ⏰ Daily, lunch and dinner

Met Fish Restaurant (££)

Popular with local families and businessmen, this unassuming clifftop fish restaurant offers delicious seafood and sea views in the popular hotel district of Lara.

✉ **Lara Yolu, Lara** ☎ 0242-321 1828 ⏰ Daily, lunch and dinner

Panoramic Restaurant (£££)

The main restaurant of the Sheraton Hotel, this is a large, brightly lit space with a terrace in summer overlooking the hotel gardens. The food includes an excellent, groaning buffet, together with *à la carte* options such as hamburgers. The hotel also has a good fish restaurant, the Maritime, and an ice cream parlour and *pâtisserie*, La Fontaine.

✉ **100 Yıl Bulvarı** ☎ 0242-243 2432 ⏰ Daily, breakfast, lunch and dinner; La Fontaine open for morning coffee, afternoon tea, and evening drinks; the Maritime open lunch and dinner, summer only

Ship Inn (££–£££)

Inside the marina, this is officially the restaurant of the Antalya Yacht Club, but it happily opens its doors to non-members. The ambience is delightful, surrounded by boats from the pretty to the mega-dream-machines, and the food, with a range of Turkish and international dishes on offer, is wonderful.

✉ **Setur Antalya Marina, Büyük Liman, Antalya Free Trade Zone** ☎ 0242-259 1290 ⏰ Daily, lunch and dinner

Sirri (££)

This attractive restaurant with a garden full of orange trees occupies a crumbling 19th-century mansion, which is also the owners' family home.

✉ **Uzunçarsı Sokak** ☎ 0242-241 7239

Sunset (££)

A welcoming restaurant with good grilled seafood.

✉ **Uzun Çarsı Sokak 19** ☎ 0242-243 9533

Yedi Mehmet (££)

The décor is dreary and, thanks to the barbecue and the usual overdose of Turkish tobacco, the atmosphere is thick with smoke, but this simple seafront restaurant provides some of the best food in town, and is a firm favourite, always packed with locals.

✉ **Konyaaltı Plajı** ☎ 0242-241 1641 ⏰ Daily, lunch and dinner

Meze

If you don't speak Turkish, don't worry. It is easy to put together a delicious meal from the *meze* (starters) which are normally laid out in a chilled cabinet. Everyone, including the Turks, wanders up for a look before deciding. Simply point to the selection of dishes you want, then add bread and salad.

Simplicity

It is hard to find a bad meal in Turkey – except in many of the massive international-style hotels and their associated clusters of over-priced restaurants, catering purely for the tourist who rates style over substance. The food is at its best when simple. Look for places where the Turks eat, and ignore the décor. Many restaurants do not serve alcohol; others allow you to bring your own for a nominal corkage; those catering primarily for tourists have a limited range of wine, beer, raki and a couple of liqueurs; only in the top restaurants and international hotels will you get a full bar service.

Aspendos

Aspendos Restaurant (££)
Popular restaurant near the ruins, with a shady terrace overlooking the river, and a good selection of Turkish specialities.
✉ On the road to the ruins ☎ 0242-735 7088 🕐 Officially open all year

Belkıs Restaurant (££)
Housed in a simple building down near the river, the food here is an imaginative selection of Turkish dishes, specialising in stews presented in attractive earthenware dishes. The wine list is also good.
✉ Belkıs Köyü, on the road to the ruins ☎ 0242-735 7263 🕐 Summer only, lunch and dinner

Duden Şelâlesi

Arkadaş Alabakık Çiftliği (£)
Charming, simple fish restaurant up a rocky track near the waterfalls. Select your trout from one of the hotel pools, then eat it beside the river. A true rural idyll.
✉ Duden Şelalesi, on the Varsak road north of Antalya 🕐 Summer only

Köprülü Kanyon

Ada Insel (£)
Stop just before you reach the canyon proper to enjoy a quiet and peaceful lunch on this shady riverside terrace, untroubled by persistent tour guides. The food is simple (fish – probably local trout – kebabs and salad) but good, and the owners friendly and unobtrusive. Rafting can be arranged from here.
✉ Köprülü Kanyon Yolu Üzeri, Beşkonak ☎ 0242-765 3389 🕐 All year, lunch and dinner

Manavgat

Gaziantep Develi Restaurant (££)
A cool oasis, right next to the waterfall, this rather scruffy-looking restaurant is immensely popular with locals, who recognise good food and a great location.
✉ Kordonboyu Caddesi ☎ 0242-746 1972 🕐 All year, lunch and dinner

Side

Afrodit Restaurant (££)
A pleasant garden terrace restaurant overlooking the yacht harbour, with a good selection of meze.
✉ Old Harbour ☎ 0242-753 1171

Liman (££)
Wonderfully situated, with an outdoor terrace beside the harbour, this seemingly simple restaurant serving a standard Turkish/international menu has a few tricks up its sleeve to ensure a thoroughly entertaining evening with excellent food. Go when you're hungry and try the towering fish platter.
✉ 71 Liman Caddesi, Side ☎ 0242-753 1168 🕐 All year, lunch and dinner

Nergiz (££)
Right on the main square beside the harbour, this is one of the smartest restaurants in town, its two storeys open-air in summer, pleasingly decorated with carpets and wicker furniture and serving a good version of the normal Turkish menu, with added lobsters.
✉ Liman Caddesi, Selimiye Köyü, Side ☎ 0242-753 1467 🕐 All year, lunch and dinner

Ockbaşi Restaurant
Away from the seafront, near the Turkish baths. A garden and children's playground add to the delicious Ottoman specialities on the menu. Vegetarian and children's menus available.
✉ Zambak Sok ☎ 0242-753 1810

Toros Motel Restaurant (££)
Good Turkish food in front of the old harbour.
✉ Liman Caddesi
☎ 0242-753 2005

Cilicia & the Hatay

Adana
Anatolian Restaurant and Bar (££)
Phoney but fun, this is a Turkish restaurant designed for Americans, with a vast buffet and seating on carpets and cushions. Owned by a man with a carpet shop; most of the clientele are American airforce personnel.
✉ Atatürk Caddesi 182, İncirlik
☎ 0322-332 8022 ⏰ All year, lunch and dinner

Mesut (££)
Attractive, spacious indoor restaurant in the quieter streets of Adana, serving an excellent version of classic Turkish food, with a wide range of *meze* and some of the best kebabs on offer.
✉ Vali Yolu Ethem, Ekin Sk, Vizon Apt Altı No 2, Adana
☎ 0322-453 3468 ⏰ All year, daily lunch and dinner

Anamur
Astor Restaurant (£)
Shady outdoor restaurant, with tables under trees, right on the beachfront, serving meze, grills and fish.
✉ İskele Mah, İnönü Caddesi, Anamur ☎ 0324-814 2280
⏰ Summer only, lunch and dinner

Çelikler/Kale (£)
The first of several small restaurants across the road from the castle, this has a pleasant, shady terrace screened by lemon trees, simple but well-cooked and presented food and a friendly host who will also transform into a tour guide and take you round the castle. There is shady parking and a small

pansiyon in summer.
✉ Mamure Kalesi Karşisi, İskele ⏰ All year, lunch and dinner

Antakya
Anadolu (££)
The décor inside and outside this old town restaurant looks like nothing, but don't be fooled – this is probably Antakya's best restaurant, with delicious food, a broad range of *meze* and a wide variety of grills and kebabs.
✉ Hurriyet Caddesi 50/C, Antakya ☎ 0326-215 1541
⏰ All year, lunch and dinner

Sultan Sofrasi (££)
Friendly, neighbourhood restaurant on the river, used as a local by many Turkish men, which offers a limited range of *meze*, some excellent soups and casseroles and, of course, kebabs.
✉ İstiklal Caddesi 18, Antakya
☎ 0326-213 8759 ⏰ All year, lunch and dinner

Mersin
Ali Baba 1 Restaurant (££)
A convenient place to eat after shopping, located by the main car park entrance.
✉ Uluçarsi Otopark Girisi Karsisi ☎ 0324-233 3088

Tarsus
Şellale (££)
This large, white building is the grandest of several restaurants and cafés surrounding the city's cooling waterfall. It is a popular venue for weddings – which perhaps explains the frilly white curtains – but the terrace overlooks the falls and the food is excellent, with a wide range of *meze*, including some unusual and delicious options. Next door is a much simpler café of the same name.
✉ Şelale, Tarsus ☎ 0324-624 8010 ⏰ All year, lunch and dinner

Too Much of a Good Thing
The aubergine or eggplant is one of the most versatile of ingredients in Turkish cookery. A careless wave at the meze counter could land you with five types of aubergine salad. During the heyday of Ottoman cuisine in the 16th century, the chefs at the court of Süleyman the Magnificent supposedly knew 150 ways of preparing them.

Lycia

Prices

The plummeting lira is proving very helpful to tourists, although up-market hotels and international tour operators continue to price in US$. Paying in lira may well prove cost-effective and you should be able to negotiate a 30–50 per cent reduction out of season. Prices in this book are divided into three categories, based on a double room with private bathroom, with a fourth to symbolise the few very expensive *de luxe* hotels in the region. Because the lira is so unstable, the categories (per room) are given in US$.

£	= US$20-40
££	= US$40-80
£££	= US$80-120 and upward

Pansiyons

The term *pansiyon* covers a huge range of smaller properties, from comfortable 20-bedroom guesthouses charging up to US$50 per room a night to a couple of barely furnished rooms sharing a bathroom at the back of someone's private home for around US$10 a night. In many ways, these offer the best, and certainly most entertaining accommodation for independent travellers, but make sure you know what you are getting.

Fethiye

Letoönia Hotel and Club (£££)

Huge, all-encompassing resort with accommodation in a large hotel block, in villas and in smaller 'club' units with wooden balconies. It also has nine bars, five restaurants, two pools, three beaches, all the land and water sports you could desire, a kids' club and a shuttle boat to Fethiye.

✉ PO Box 63, 48300 Fethiye-Muğla; 3km from Fethiye ☎ 0252-614 4966, fax: 0252-614 4422 ☼ All year, but restricted facilities in winter

Villa Daffodil (££)

This small, quiet, Ottoman-style *pansiyon* has attractive rooms, a pool, a sauna and a restaurant; 1 km from the town centre. Early booking essential.

✉ Fevzi Çakmak Caddesi 115 Karagözler ☎ 0242-614 9595, fax: 0242-612 2223 ☼ Summer only

Kalkan

Club Patara/Patara Prince (£££)

This is the most luxurious resort in the area, with a five-star hotel and an estate of timeshare houses, all designed by top Turkish architect Turhan Kaşo. Facilities include tennis courts, a scuba centre, Italian restaurant, shops etc.

✉ 5km from the village centre ☎ 0242-844 3920, fax: 0242-844 3930 ☼ Some sections open all year

Pirat Otel (££)

A medium-sized resort hotel right in the village, its pool deck and balconies overlooking the harbour.

✉ Kalkan Marina ☎ 0242-844 3178, fax: 0242-844 3183 ☼ Summer only

Kaş

Aquapark Hotel (£££)

The resort's largest and finest hotel, at the end of the peninsula, about 3km from the town centre, with fabulous views, pool, restaurants, disco and water-slides. Also runs the smaller Aquapark Twins.

✉ Çukurbağ Yarımadası ☎ 0242-836 1901, fax: 0242-836 1992 ☼ All year

Arpia Pansiyon (££)

Charming, quiet *pansiyon* on the peninsula, with its own pool and restaurant.

✉ Çukurbağ Yarımadası ☎ 0242-836 2642, fax: 0242-836 3163 ☼ Summer only

Hera Hotel (£££)

Wonderfully grandiose, neo-classical hotel right on the seafront, within walking distance of the town centre. Each of the 40 rooms has a balcony and the hotel also has a Turkish bath, sauna, jacuzzi, fitness centre, disco, games room and shopping mall. The pool deck leads on to a private beach.

✉ Küçükçakil Mevcii, Kaş ☎ 0242-836 3062, fax: 0242-836 3063 ☼ All year

Hotel Club Phellos (££)

Central, modern 3-star holiday hotel. Architecture and furnishings are a little spartan, but the 80 rooms all have balconies with sea views and there is a good pool and sauna.

✉ Doğruyol Sk, Kaş ☎ 0242-836 1953, fax: 0242-836 1890 ☼ All year

Kemer

Most of the hotels in Kemer itself are small and modest; the giants are stretched out along Göynük beach, about 9km east. Other satellite resorts include Beldibi, Tekirova and Çamyuva.

Hotel Kaliptus (££)

Small, friendly and attractive hotel with a pool and two restaurants, within easy reach of the town centre and beach.

✉ Main road into Kemer ☎ 0242-814 2467 🕐 Summer only

Royal Resort Hotel (£££)

One of the smallest and most luxurious of the string of giant resorts along this hotel strip. This one has 187 rooms, all with balconies, nine villas and four on-site restaurants, as well as the pool, sauna, bars, shops and other necessities.

✉ Göynük, Kemer ☎ 0242-815 2370, fax: 0242-815 1627 🕐 All year

Sultan Saray (£££)

This vast, cube-like complex of nearly 500 rooms, built around a courtyard, is one of a growing number of 'all-inclusive' resorts, which even include your beer, wine and snacks as part of the package. Everything is laid on, from lavish buffets to six bars, tennis and squash courts, pools for adults and children (heated outdoor and indoor), water sports, films, cabaret, a private beach, a health club – the list goes on. The hotel is comfortable and efficient.

✉ Göynük, Kemer ☎ 0242-815 1480, fax: 0242-815 1499 🕐 All year

Ölüdeniz

Club Belcekiz Beach (££)

Attractively colourful, low-rise holiday village in the village centre, right on the beach and within easy walking distance of the lagoon. Facilities include a pool and jacuzzi, shopping mall, Turkish bath, pizzeria and Chinese restaurant.

✉ Ölüdeniz 48300, Fethiye-Muğla ☎ 0252-616 6009, fax: 0252-616 6448 🕐 Summer only

Hotel Montana Pine Resort (£££)

Set in the pine forests in the hills overlooking the lagoon, this is a charming hotel with low-rise blocks of rooms with wooden balconies, scattered through shady gardens. There are three pools, tennis courts, a gym and games room and a shuttle bus to the beach.

✉ Ovacık Mah, Ölüdeniz Beldesi, Fethiye ☎ 0252-616 7108, fax: 0252-616 6451 🕐 Summer only

Patara

Beyhan Hotel (£££)

Large, attractive resort hotel with a large pool, on the hill overlooking Patara beach.

✉ Iskata Mev ☎ 0242-843 5098, fax: 0242-843 5097 🕐 All year

Patara View Hotel (£)

Charming, small *pansiyon* set on a ridge just east of town, with a barbecue terrace, fine views and shuttle service to the beach. The same management also runs the Golden, which has the best restaurant in the village.

✉ Gelimiş Köyü ☎ 0242-843 5184, fax: 0242-843 5022 🕐 Summer only

Reading the Stars

Star-ratings are based purely on the availability of facilities, not on atmosphere or maintenance. In general, expect everything to be a category below its western European or American level (eg a Turkish 4-star will be at the level of an average British 3-star).

What to Expect

With 175,000 beds available on the coast, and more hotels and *pansiyons* opening every season, there is no shortage of accommodation along the Turkish south coast. The huge majority, however, is either soulless or basic, or both. Very few hotels have real character, but equally, very few are disastrously bad. In summer, check that there is air-conditioning; in winter, check that there is central heating (many cheaper places have neither, and both are necessary). Even more importantly, check that there is hot water; many places rely on solar energy to heat the water to a pleasant tepid in summer, but it remains numbingly cold in winter. Take your own plug for basins and baths.

103

Pamphylia, Cilicia & the Hatay

Hotels in Alanya
The main hotel strip for Alanya is about 20km west of the city, along İnçekum beach, where there are at least 20 large hotels, with more still under construction.

Pamphylia

Alanya
Bedesten (££)
Converted 13th-century Selçuk caravansaray on the castle rock, with superb views and pool.

✉ İçkale, Alanya ☎ 0242-512 1234, fax: 0242-513 7934 🕐 All year

Club Green Fuğla Beach (££)
One of the most attractive of the large resort hotels along the İnçekum beach strip, with simple balcony rooms in brightly painted low-rise blocks, round the pool, bar and shops. With a friendly staff, this is a good stop, as long as you are prepared to eat out.

✉ İnçekum Fuğla Köyü, Avsallar ☎ 0242-517 2870, fax: 0242-517 2543 🕐 All year

Kaptan (££)
Small, friendly and well-positioned near the Kizil Kule, this is an ideal city centre base.

✉ İskele Caddesi 70 ☎ 0242-513 4900, fax: 0242-513 2000 🕐 All year

Antalya
Dedekonak (£)
Simply restored *konak* (mansion) that offers a rare opportunity for good, cheap lodging in an old city historic house. There is a courtyard with a marble fountain.

✉ Kılıçarslan Mahallesi, Hıdırlık Sokak 13 ☎ 0242-247 5170, fax: 0242-247 5170 🕐 All year

Falez (£££)
A large, luxury hotel, right beside the Sheraton on Antalya's beach strip, the 5-star Falez has 320 rooms, all with seaview balconies, adults' and children's pools, and offers a variety of water and beach sports including tennis, sailing, windsurfing, water-skiing, aerobics, riding, volley ball and archery.

✉ Konyaaltı Falez Mekvii, 07050 Antalya ☎ 0242-248 5000, fax: 0242-248 5025 🕐 All year

Sheraton Voyager (£££)
Probably the finest hotel on the Turkish Riviera, the Sheraton, on the Konyaalti beachfront just outside central Antalya, happily combines its roles as business hotel and luxury holiday resort. The standard is up to the usual Sheraton excellence, there are several good restaurants and bars and, as an added bonus, there are attractive gardens, with a jogging track and a huge pool, and a full-blown health centre and gym.

✉ 100 Yil Bulvari, 07050 Antalya ☎ 0242-243 2432, fax: 0242-243 2462 🕐 All year

Tütav Türk Evi Otelleri (£££)
This delightful, sumptuously furnished small hotel, with 20 rooms, was created from three lovingly restored Ottoman mansions in the heart of the old town. The hotel stretches out along the fortress walls with magnificent views from the bar, restaurant and pool deck.

✉ Mermerli Sok 2, 07100 Kaleiçi ☎ 0242-248 6591, fax: 0242-241 9419 🕐 All year

Aspendos
Attaleia (£££)
Glamorous and luxurious

holiday village set in mature landscaped gardens, amidst the pine forests, right on the beach. Restaurants, bars, fitness centre, pools and many sporting facilities, including a golf course.

✉ **Belek** ☎ **0242-725 4301, fax: 0242-725 4324** 🕒 **All year**

Side

Hanimeli Pansiyon (£)

Tiny, delightful hotel with a marble staircase and garden courtyard. Town centre.

✉ **Turgut Reis Sok** ☎ **0242-753 1789** 🕒 **Summer only**

Side Palace Hotel (£££)

Huge, white-winged resort on the beach, with six bars, two restaurants, pools, a health club, water and land sports and all the other trimmings expected of a top resort.

✉ **Sorgun Mevkii** ☎ **0242-756 9321, fax: 0242-756 9320** 🕒 **All year**

Cilicia & the Hatay

Adana

Hotel Seyhan (£££)

Adana's premier hotel, a glittering, mirror-plated tower in the town centre, with all the trimmings – a swimming pool, a health club, a nightclub and five bars.

✉ **Turhan Cemal Beriker Bulv 30, 01120 Adana** ☎ **0322-457 5810, fax: 0322-454 2834**

Inci Hotel (££)

Large, city-centre, business-style hotel with well-appointed rooms, friendly and helpful staff, and a bar, a nightclub, a beautician and a sauna in the basement.

✉ **Kurtuluş Caddesi 40, 01060 Kuruköprü, Adana** ☎ **0322-435 8234, fax: 0322-435 8368** 🕒 **All year**

Anamur

Hotel Hermes (££)

Friendly, simply but well-furnished seaside hotel with central heating, air-conditioning, a swimming pool and a sauna. All rooms have balconies. In season, the disco can be noisy.

✉ **İskele Mevkii 33006, Anamur** ☎ **0324-814 3950, fax: 0324-814 3995** 🕒 **All year**

Yalı Motel (£)

Attractive, seafront motel right on the beach, with 16 simple en suite bungalows, camping and caravan space in shady gardens, and an on-site restaurant and café-bar. Booking advised.

✉ **Yalı Mah, İskele, Anamur** ☎ **0324-814 1435, fax: 0324-814 3474** 🕒 **Summer only**

Antakya

Büyük Antakya Oteli (£££)

Very centrally located, beside the river and within easy walking distance of the old town, this is Antakya's best hotel: comfortable, smart and friendly – although its furnishings and services drag a little behind its 4-star prices.

✉ **Atatürk Caddesi 8, 31040 Antakya** ☎ **0326-213 5860, fax: 0326-213 5869** 🕒 **All year**

Mersin

Hilton (£££)

Twelve storeys of gleaming American-style modernity with Mediterranean views.

✉ **Adnan Menderes Bulv 3310** ☎ **0324 326 5000, fax: 0324-326 5050** 🕒 **All year**

Tarsus

Mersin Oteli (£££)

Large, modern hotel, well situated on the edge of the city, near the waterfall. The rooms are spacious and well-decorated, the service is well-meaning and the food is less than inspiring. Luckily there is an excellent restaurant within walking distance.

✉ **Şelale, Tarsus** ☎ **0324-614 0600, fax: 0324-614 0033** 🕒 **All year**

Hotels in Antalya

There are numerous small hotels and pansiyons in the old town and a few larger properties facing Konyaaltı Beach, but most of Antalya's larger hotels and package tour properties are in Lara, a modern suburb along the seafront about 10km east of the city. A local speciality is the growing number of Special Licence hotels, small up-market properties in restored historic houses.

Carpets & Leather

Bargain Buying

All shops in Turkey expect you to bargain, a leisurely, entertaining activity involving comfortable seats, pleasant conversation and ubiquitous glasses of tea. Prices start significantly higher in summer, and many places automatically quote in US dollars or Deutschmarks. The price often tumbles if you pay in Turkish lira. Persistence should mean a reduction of 30–50 per cent.

Carpets

Magnificent carpets, from cushion covers to full room size, have been made in Turkey for the last 8,000 years. The best are wool on wool, wool on cotton, silk on cotton or silk on silk. In tufted carpets, the wool should be double-knotted for strength; the more knots per square inch, the better the quality. Flat-weave *kilims* derive from the nomadic traditions, while *sumaks*, *kilims* with a further pattern embroidered on top, usually come from the Kurdish and Turkistan areas. Check the quality and be careful about old carpets – many are aged with the help of tea and sunlight. Good shops will provide a certificate of authenticity and handle shipping.

Alanya
Candan Carpets
A branch of an Istanbul company with a huge stock and knowledgeable staff.
- ✉ **Müftüler Caddesi 9/E**
- ☎ **0242-512 6020**

Motif Kilim House
Large quantities of carpet at a range of qualities and prices. Beware of the machine-made offerings.
- ✉ **Hükümet Caddesi, Üçüncü Sokak 8** ☎ **0242-513 0923**

Antalya
Antik Bazaar
Established, reliable stockist of a broad range of fine carpets and *kilims*.
- ✉ **Selçuk Mah, İzmirli Ali Efendi Sokak, 12**

Bazaar 54
With 11 branches, Bazaar 54 is the world's largest retailer of Turkish carpets, buying direct from and, in some cases, employing the producers. You can pay a deposit, with the balance due only when your carpet arrives safely at your home.
- ✉ **Yat Limanı, Kaleiçi 4**
- ☎ **0242-241 0290**

Galeri Sumak
One of the most sumptuous of the old town carpet shops, with a refreshingly leisurely sales pitch.
- ✉ **Tuzcular Mahallesi Paşa Cami Sokak 18, Kaleiçi**
- ☎ **0242-247 2143**

Aspendos
Bazaar 54
Right next to the jewellery centre, Bazaar 54 is a huge, upmarket shopping centre, originally part of Turkey's foremost chain of carpet retailers (see Antalya), but also with large jewellery and leather shops. Carpets are woven on site.
- ✉ **Küçükbelkıs Köyü 07506, Serik** ☎ **0242-735 7281**
- ⏲ **Daily 9-6**

Fethiye
Old Orient Kilim Bazaar
Sumptuous *kilim* shop in a restored Ottoman house.
- ✉ **Karagözler Caddesi 5**
- ☎ **0252-612 1059**

Kaş
One of the best shopping centres on the coast, with an excellent range of carpets, jewellery and designer fashion. There is a big market on Fridays behind the bus station on the Elmalı road.

Kaş and Carry
Two branches of the same excellent carpet shop, selling work from its own co-

operative and elsewhere.
✉ **Uzunçarşı Orta Sokak 6**
☎ **0242-836 1663** ✉ **Bahçe Sokak** ☎ **0242- 836 1662**

Magic Orient
Both branches of this shop are Aladdin's caves of richly patterned silk and wool, with carpets, *kilims* and *sumaks*.
✉ **Cumhuriyet Meydanı 7**
☎ **0242-836 1610** ✉ **Hükümet Caddesi 15** ☎ **0242-836 3150**

Perge
Golden Perge Shopping Centre
Huge, tourist-targeted sales emporium with a dazzling selection of carpets and jewellery for those with hefty credit limits.
✉ **Aksu, 10 km east of Antalya, near Perge turn-off**

Side
Merve Halı Galeri
Well-stocked carpet shop; try some serious bargaining.
✉ **Köy Meydanı** ☎ **0242-753 2029**

Nomad Carpet Centre
Main street carpet emporium, one of several competing ferociously for the tourist's custom.
✉ **Liman Caddesi** ☎ **0242-753 1451**

Leather
Leather goods are around third of their Northern European price, half what you would pay in the US. Top of the range are trendy leather coats and jackets, and beautifully designed and made handbags and wallets. Shoes generally do not keep up with Western fashion and there is also a great deal of junk at inflated prices.

Alanya
Lederland
Massive stock and reasonable prices make this a good hunting ground for leather-lovers.

✉ **İskele Caddesi 6/B**
☎ **0242-513 9613**

Nihan Leather
Another large outlet, specialising in brightly coloured fashion items.
✉ **Keykubat Caddesi 29**
☎ **0242-513 2031**

Antalya
Matraş
Long established leather manufacturer, producing excellent bags, briefcases and wallets.
✉ **Cumhuriyet Caddesi 58/B**
☎ **0242-240 3042**

Punto Leather Production Centre
Excellent leather workshop producing high fashion jackets, belts, bags and luggage. The shopping experience includes a tour of the workshop and there are also Levis and Wranglers at factory outlet prices.
✉ **Doğu Yaka Mah, Gazi Bulv. 1, Orman Fidanlığı Karsısı**
☎ **0242-321 7309**

Kaş
Premier Leather Collection
A wide range of clothes and accessories, using soft, brightly coloured leathers for high fashion designs.
✉ **Şube Sokak**

Marmaris
Duygu Bag Shop
Quality leather travel bags, handbags, belts and briefcases in this bazaar shop. There is a similar kind of shop at the other end of the pedestrianised passageway, so compare products and prices.
✉ **Tepe Mah Rıhtım Sokak 11/A** ☎ **0252-412 8117**

Stock Leather
Handbags, belts, wallets, purses, suitcases and designer-label items.
✉ **Kenan Evren Caddesi 2/K, Marmaris**

VAT Refunds
Tourists may obtain a tax refund from authorised retailers on any purchases over 5,000,000TL. Ask for three signed and validated copies of your receipt. Some retailers may refund the tax on the spot. Others should give you a voucher which can either be reclaimed from a bank or desk within the customs area of larger airports or posted back within one month of returning home. Check the exact procedure followed by each shop. If buying antiques of any kind, including carpets or jewellery, you must have an export clearance certificate from a museum or the Ministry of Antiquities.

Jewellery, Fashion, Books & Gifts

Shopping in Adana
The heartland of tourist shopping is about 25km east of Adana, outside the huge Inçerlik American airforce base, where a whole village of souvenir shops has mushroomed. Everything is priced (expensively) in dollars, but there are some good shops. Best buys include a wide range of copper, brass, pewter and onyx, excellent leather jackets and handbags, custom-designed satin quilts, carpets and jewellery.

Jewellery
Hidden amongst a sea of mass-market tat are some true delights, with delicate hand-worked chains, exquisite traditional filigree, and even a few genuine antiques. The craft is Turkish, but almost all the stones are imported. A few key centres produce magnificent, custom-designed pieces literally fit for kings. Prices are reasonable, but if you are serious about buying, do some homework before leaving home. Otherwise, window-shopping is fun.

Alanya
Akman Jewellery
Gold, silver, precious and semi-precious stones are all on sale in this solid jewellers. Good quality, but few surprises.
✉ **Hükümet Caddesi 62**
☎ **0242-513 3287**

Gold Paradise
In this case, all that glitters is gold – all finely worked and lovely to hold.
✉ **Bostancıpınarı Caddesi 12**
☎ **0242-513 9839**

Tiffany
One of the largest and best known shops in a strip of up-market jewellers. No relation to the New York version.
✉ **Hükümet Caddesi 44**
☎ **0242-512 1069**

Antalya
Dösem
Ministry of Culture souvenir shop, with an excellent collection of fine handicrafts from across Turkey, including reproduction ancient jewellery. Other branches at Antalya museum and Aspendos.
✉ **Yacht Harbour, 24**
☎ **0242-241 4667**

Aspendos
Aspendos Jewellery Centre
This vast jewellery empire on the approach road to Aspendos is a dazzling sea of magnificent gold, silver and precious stones. The experience begins with a tour of the ground floor workshops, with 180 jewellers working on site (the stones are behind glass); followed by tea and courteous persuasion amidst acres of gleaming cases. Options range from simple charms and silver cartouches with your name in Hittite, to solitaire rocks and custom-designed splendour. Worth a stop even if not buying.
✉ **Küçükbelkıs Köyü 07506, Serik** ☎ **0242-735 7250**

Fethiye
Talisman Jewellery
Shopping choices in Fethiye are limited and this little shop has one of the better selections of gold, silver and precious stones. Mostly necklaces, rings, bangles and ornate earrings; nothing is terribly expensive. Also carries out repairs.
✉ **Hamam Sokak 15/1, Fethiye**
☎ **0252 614 8585**

Kaş
Argentum
Silver specialists with antique and modern jewellery and plate.
✉ **Uzunçarşı Caddesi 19**
☎ **0242-836 2664**

Topika
Stunning designs in silver and precious stones, with a

custom-design service on offer.

📧 **Bahçe Sokak** 📞 **0242-836 2363**

Xtra Kuyumcular

Innovative contemporary design, much of it based on Lycian originals. The perfect souvenir for the style-conscious with cash.

📧 **Elmalı Caddesi** 📞 **0242-836 2372**

Side

Flash Jewellery

Tiny backstreet jeweller with wonderful imaginative gold and precious stones worked into pieces designed by the owner.

📧 **Liman Caddesi** 📞 **0242-753 2519**

Jasmin Jewellery

Wide-ranging stock and helpful staff, eager to make use of your credit card.

📧 **Liman Caddesi 56** 📞 **0242-753 2258**

Fashion, Books & Gifts

Antalya

Ardıc Kitabevi

Stocks foreign language books, magazines and newspapers.

📧 **Selekler Çarşısı, 67**
📞 **0242-247 0356**

Fethiye

Fethiye has an excellent daily market, between Çarşı Caddesi and Tütün Sok (mainly food, but some souvenirs and lots of good-quality fakes), which swells to impressive dimensions when the local villagers arrive on Tuesdays.

Imagine

Excellent bookshop, with a large supply of English-language novels and guides, plus music.

📧 **Cumhuriyet Caddesi 9**
📞 **0252-614 8465**

Kaş

Butik Sera

Casual fun with style is the watchword here. The owner, Hatice, will custom-design and make clothes for you if you have the time.

📧 **Bahçe Sokak** 📞 **0242-836 2426**

Gonca Spice Shop

Spices, teas, essential oils and souvenirs.

📧 **Bahçe Sokak 3** 📞 **0242-836 2377**

Papilio Butik

Owner-designer Sumru goes way back to the region's roots, specialising in gorgeous, free-flowing Grecian-style dresses, many made of locally handloomed fabrics.

📧 **Bahçe Sokak** 📞 **0242-836 2895**

Tufan Designer

The local tailor has branched out into fashion, with silk tunics and harem pants for women, as well as custom-designed menswear.

📧 **Şube Sokak** 📞 **0242-836 2917**

Marmaris

Continental

Dedicated solely to Turkish ceramics, mostly plates and vases: some of the hand-painted work is quite beautiful. Packaging is provided. Easy to find, in the bazaar.

📧 **Eski Carsi Sokak 28/A**
📞 **0252-413 4008**

Nur-Bal

Bring home a jar or two of Marmaris honey. This little shop, in a block behind the post office, has a good selection. The dark-coloured, black-pine honey is a local speciality, but also ask to see some *portakal*, a light-coloured and very sweet variation.

📧 **Fevzi Paça Caddesi 9/C**

Shopping in Antalya

Much of the old town is now wall-to-wall carpet, jewellery and ceramic shops, divided only by trendy fashion boutiques, small cafés and *pansiyons* and sellers of beads and fake Cartier and Gucci watches. Brave the often very aggressive sales pitches and allow yourself time to browse and make up your mind. There is a big daily general market, the Halk Pazar, next to the municipal bus terminus.

Children's Activities

What to Eat

Formula and powdered baby food are easily available, but the bottled variety is not, and it may be worth bringing a stock of your own. The milk is safe, as is fruit juice, although tap water is not. Impress on your children that even teeth should be cleaned with bottled water. For older children, the Turkish diet is simple and very healthy and there should be few problems, except with vegetarians.

Caves

Alanya

Dalmataş Mağarası
The 'Weeping Cave' (► 59) is a magical place to take children, with its eerie stalactites and stalagmites.
✉ **South end of western beach**
🕐 **Daily 10–8**

Rides and Waterparks

Antalya

Aqualand
Just behind Konyaaltı Beach, this large waterpark has recently re-opened after major renovations, with added slides.
✉ **Dumlupinar Bulvari**
☎ **0242-243 4544**
💶 **Expensive**

Aquapark
The better of Antalya's two waterparks, beautifully set on the cliff top in front of the Dedeman Hotel. There are several high, long, looping waterslides for the more adventurous, gentle versions for small children and several pools and jacuzzis for the staid.
✉ **Hotel Dedeman, Lara Yolu**
☎ **0242-321 7938**
💶 **Expensive**

Speedland Gokart Centre
Large karting track, popular with local youths; just out of town on the airport road.
✉ **Alanya Road** ☎ **0242-248 3945** 💶 **Expensive**

Lunapark Funfair
Traditional funfair, with merry-go-rounds, rides and plastic prizes. A severe let-down for children raised on Western theme parks, but a good way of filling an evening.
✉ **Konyaaltı** ☎ **0242-247 6889** 💶 **Expensive**

Kemer

Aquaworld
Definitely the little brother of the Antalya parks, this seafront operation has a couple of smallish slides and pools.
✉ **İskele Caddesi (seafront)**
🕐 **Daily 9.30–6.30**
💶 **Expensive**

Naturland Country Park
The one and only theme park on the coast, a gentle place dedicated to the countryside with an organic farm, animals to pet, a children's playhouse, demonstrations of making cheese, ayran, bread and pasta, a monorail to some waterfalls, bowls and billiards, a café and a restaurant.
✉ **Çamyuva, 8km south of Kemer, off the N-400** ☎ **0242-824 6214** 🕐 **Daily 9–6**
💶 **Expensive**

Marmaris

Atlantis Aquapark & Aquapark Içmeler
The Atlantis Aquapark is a recently opened water-based fun park for children, consisting mainly of various slides and a froggy island and bunny slides for small children. There's also a beach bar for bored parents. Aquapark Içmeler, under the same management, has been around a bit longer and it is easy to find, on the right as one enters Içmeler from Marmaris.
✉ **Marmaris and Içmeler**
☎ **0252-413 0308 and 0252-455 5049** 🕐 **Morning to night**
💶 **Expensive**

Evening Entertainment

Much of the evening entertainment along southern Turkey's coastal strip is laid on purely for tourists, and while the place is humming in summer, it is like a ghost town out of season. Many previously popular venues have shut because of the recent law banning casinos.

Alanya
Auditorium Open Air Disco
Loud, brash but buzzing open air disco.
✉ Dimçayi Mevkii

Janus Restaurant and Café-Bar
Bright (pink), noisy and cheerful all day, churning out food and drink, from kebabs to burgers and pizzas, with late-night dancing.
✉ Rıhtım Girişi (near the harbour) ☎ 0242-513 2694

Antalya
Birdland Jazz Club
Cool and trendy jazz club in a restored *konak* (mansion), with a breezy terrace overlooking the sea.
✉ Hıdırlık Kulesi Arkası, Hesapçı Sokak, 78 Kaleiçi ☎ 0242-242 01507

Çizgi Café and Bar
The yachting world meets Turkish kitsch in this old town bar, where you can lounge on cushions near low tables like an Ottoman potentate, surrounded by nautical memorabilia. Serves good cocktails and some snacks.
✉ Uzun Çarşı 28, Kaleiçi ☎ 0242-248 1549

Club 29
Right down on the water's edge in the old town

harbour, this upmarket restaurant transforms itself later in the evening into a huge disco (open-air and indoor). It also has a large pool and some live performances by top Turkish bands.
✉ Yat Liman, Kaleiçi ☎ 0242-241 6260 ⏱ year round, disco in summer only

No Name Bar
Lively and noisy party bar in the old marina with live American rock and roll and karaoke in nine languages. There are also an Internet café, satellite TV, an English-language library and regular theme nights.
✉ Old Marina, Antalya ☎ 0242-241 0538

PM Bar and Underground
Head here if you are young, have too much energy and like deafening noise. The blaring music is rock and Turkish pop, the place is jammed and the alcohol flows free.
✉ Cumhuriyet Caddesi 59, Sokak 8 ☎ 0242-247 3256

Fethiye
Disco Marina
Popular disco with mirror balls on the ceiling and belly-dancing amongst the entertainments; popular with the young crowd. Air conditioned.
✉ Birinci Karagözler, Yat Limanı Karsısı ☎ 0252-614 9860

Otantik Bar
More mirror balls and plenty of noise to shake the structure of this restored Ottoman house.
✉ Paspatur Mevkii Hamam Sokak ☎ 0252-614 6954

Dancing
All the resorts have discos or disco-bars, some open-air, a short way out of town. None is expensive; most are loud, with a mixed crowd of locals and tourists. Almost all the big hotels also have their own discos, and many also have a slightly more sophisticated nightclub with live entertainment. These are almost entirely touristy, as few local Turks can afford the price of the drinks. Antalya has a few more stylish cocktail bars with live jazz or piano music. Nowhere is expensive and most places stay open until 3.30AM, or until the last customers leave. Few stay open in winter.

Film
There are cinemas in all the major towns, and some even show their first-run Hollywood films in English. Most of the resort hotels have a programme of films in German, French and, occasionally, English, while a few backstreet cafés offer films dubbed into Turkish for the locals.

Ottoman
It is a little surprising there aren't more pubs like this one along the coast. The interior re-creates, with some imagination, an Ottoman-style atmosphere with the help of antique copper pots adorning the walls and Turkish folk music that conjures up a dance of whirling dervishes. The place is sometimes taken over by package groups, brought here by tour operators, but it can make a relaxing venue during the afternoon or early evening. Beer, cocktails and *raki* served until the not-so-early hours of the morning. The water pipes on display are for sale.
✉ Karagözler Caddesi 3/B
☎ 0252-612 1148

Kalkan
Aquarium Bar
The place to hang out in town, with three floors of entertainment, including a lively bar, excellent music, games, billiards room, and live shows with transvestite belly-dancers!
✉ Town centre ☎ 0242-844 3453

Kaş
Fullmoon Disco/MDC
Two popular, seafront open-air discos, both sited a short way out of town.
✉ Fullmoon Hotel, 1km out of town on Kalkan road ☎ 0242-836 3241; MDC ✉ MDC, 1km east of town on the Demre road ☎ 0242-836 2491

Genç Club Café-Bar & Sun Café
Two bars, both decorated with cushions and carpets, providing havens of calm away from the heaving throng. The décor is delightful, the atmosphere soothing, with some quiet Turkish music.
Genç Club ✉ Ilkokul Caddesi ☎ 0242-836 3060
Sun Café ✉ In the harbour, near the Elit Bar

Kemer
Ayışığı Disco
A thumpingly loud and always crowded disco serving everything from rock to jazz.
✉ Moonlight Park, near the marina ☎ 0242-814 3250

Marmaris & İçmeler
Joy
This is a well-established disco in İçmeler and its circular shape makes it easy to identify, situated on the right side of the main road as one comes into İçmeler from Marmaris.
✉ İçmeler ☎ 0252-455 3302
🚍 *Dolmuş* to Marmaris

Beach Club
An indoor disco with DJs providing the music and occasional appearances by professional singers. Very popular and currently the 'in' place.
✉ Uzunyale Marmaris

Side
Blues Bar
Warm, friendly bar with an outdoor terrace serving 100 different cocktails.
✉ Cami Sokak ☎ 0242-753 1197

Zeppelin Bar
Loud music, large crowds, a hot, sweaty atmosphere and sea views. Great if you like that sort of thing.
✉ Barbaros Caddesi, 68
☎ 0242-753 4323

Tours & Activities

Sightseeing Tours

One of the easiest ways to get out and about on the Turkish South Coast is to take one of the many half-day, day or short-break tours on offer. Numerous options cover activities from *gület* trips to beach barbecues, intensive history to cultural extravaganzas, visiting nomad encampments to jeep safaris. Walk along the quay and hop on to any one of a dozen boats, or visit one of the many travel agents in the resorts. Do a little homework first to stop yourself being pressurised into a hasty decision and high price by the over-eager salesmen. Few tours operate in winter, but someone will always take you if you have the cash. Just ask around.

Adana
Adalı Turizm
Full travel agency service.
✉ **Stadyum Caddesi 37/C**
☎ **0322-453 7440**

Alanya
Avira Travel Agency
Sightseeing, yacht charters and jeep safaris.
✉ **Saray Mahallesi, Ataturk Caddesi 8** ☎ **0242-512 6191**

Antalya
Akay Travel Service
Tours to hard-to-reach archaeological sights.
✉ **Cumhuriyet Caddesi 54**
☎ **0242-243 1700**

Pamfilya
Sightseeing, yacht charters, rafting, and trekking.
✉ **30 Ağustos Caddesi 57/B**
☎ **0242-243 1500/242 1404**

Skorpion Turizm
Sightseeing, mountaineering, jeep safaris, trekking, and village tours.
✉ **Fevzi Çakmak Caddesi 26/A**
☎ **0242-241 6938**

Stop Tours
Mountain biking, horse-riding, yacht tours and historic sights.
✉ **Dr Burhanettin Onat Caddesi, Yılmaz Sitesi, A Blok, No. 14** ☎ **0242-322 6557**

Tantur
Sightseeing tours, diving, along with yacht and helicopter charter.
✉ **Atatürk Caddesi 31**
☎ **0242-426 2530**

Fethiye
Light Tours
General travel agent organising everything from sightseeing to cruises or jeep safaris.
✉ **Atatürk Caddesi 104**
☎ **0252-614 4757**

Simena Travel
Sightseeing, island and moonlight cruises, jeep safaris.
✉ **Atatürk Caddesi, PTT Santral Sokak, Urantaş Sitesi, Kat 4** ☎ **0252-614 4957**

Kalkan
Adda Tour and Travel Agency
Provides sightseeing, cruises, diving, villa and car rentals.
✉ **Yalıboyu Mahallesi**
☎ **0242-844 3610**

Kaş
Bougainville Travel
Cultural sightseeing guided by experts, along with boat tours, trekking and nomadic village safaris.
✉ **Çukurbağlı Caddesi 10**
☎ **0242-836 3142**

Emergencies

There is no need to worry as long as you take sensible precautions. Turkey is basically hygienic and civilised, with good standards of medical care. Children should keep on their hats (against the sun) and shoes (against nasty insects and bits of broken glass), use sunblock, drink plenty of liquids, wash their hands regularly and watch where they put them when scrambling around on the rocks (look out for scorpions or snakes). Take plenty of pills to counteract the inevitable travel sickness on the twisting roads. Ideally, avoid July and August, when the heat is often unbearable and the crowds are at their rowdiest.

The Tourist Trail
Many big hotels are almost exclusively occupied by package tourists, who arrive on charters and live beside the swimming pool and bar for two weeks. Along the Mediterranean, from Antalya to Alanya, most are German. Kaş and Fethiye attract a multinational crowd, and west of Fethiye is almost exclusively British. Relatively few foreigners ever stray east of Alanya. If socialising with other tourists is a priority, check carefully when booking.

Rekor Tourism and Travel Agency
Tours to Kekova, the mountain villages, Castellorizo and trekking.
✉ Cumhuriyet Meydanı
☎ 0242-836 1725

Kemer
Akay
Excursions to local archaeological sites.
✉ Liman Caddesi ☎ 0242-814 4890

Pamfilya Tour
Local branch of the nationwide operator.
✉ Hastane Caddesi 122, Sokak 21/B ☎ 0242-814 1981

Mersin
Bumer Tourism and Travel Agency
Sightseeing excursions, car rental, transfers and ticketing.
✉ Palmiye Mahallesi İsmet İnönü Bulv, Merkon Sitesi N Blok 5 ☎ 0324-326 6271

Side
Şelale Tour
Local day trips and regional excursions.
✉ Liman Caddesi ☎ 0242-753 1066

Sporting Tours
Most large beach hotels run their own programmes of water sports and either have or provide access to tennis courts, but inland adventure sports such as riding, trekking and whitewater rafting are also growing in popularity. In winter, there is skiing in the Taurus Mountains, a short way inland. Turkey's premier golf course is at Belek, near Aspendos, with access from all the large local hotels, many of which also have their own courses. Some of the general travel agents and tour operators listed above also offer a variety of sporting activities.

Alanya
Alraft Rafting and Riding Club
Whitewater rafting on the Dimçay river and riding expeditions in nearby forests.
✉ Biçakçı Köyü Mevkii
☎ 0242-513 9155 ✉ Azak Hotel, Alanya ☎ 0242-512 3966

Active Divers
Diving tours, underwater photography and PADI (Professional Association of Diving Instructors) courses, from the Pasha Bay Hotel.
✉ İskele Caddesi 80 ☎ 0242-512 8811

Martin Türkay
Mountain and motor bikes for hire.
✉ Atatürk Caddesi 95/C
☎ 0242-513 5666

Antalya
Medraft
Whitewater rafting trips in the Köprülü Kanyon.
✉ Konyaalti Caddesi, Derya Apartmanı A Blok, 68/16
☎ 0242-248 0083

Skorpion Turizm
Mountaineering, hiking and jeep safaris are among the activities on offer.
✉ Fevzi Çakmak Caddesi 26/A
☎ 0242-241 6938

Stop Tours
Yatching, horse-riding and mountain biking for the energetic holiday-makers.
✉ Dr Burhanettin Onat Caddesi, Yılmaz Sitesi, A Blok, No. 14 ☎ 0242-322 6557

Trek Travel
Climbing and trekking expeditions locally, and longer excursions to other parts of Turkey.
✉ Kızılsaray Mahallesi, 61 Sokak Alanya İş Merkezi 10-16
☎ 0242-248 1629

Fethiye and Ölüdeniz
There are numerous

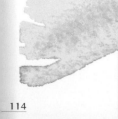

opportunities here for all sorts of sport, from water sports on the Ölüdeniz lagoon to paragliding off 1,975m-high Mount Babadagi, rafting on the Dalaman and Esen rivers and walking, riding and jeep safaris in the mountains.

European Diving Center
British-run company offering courses and daily dives; PADI.
✉ **Atatürk Caddesi** ☎ **0252-614 9771**

Explora
Jeep safaris, water sports, parascending, scuba diving, horse-riding and excursions to Rhodes.
✉ **Hisarönü, Fethiye** ☎ **0252-616 6890**
✉ **Han Camp, Ölüdeniz** ☎ **0252-616 6316**

Natur Travel Agency
Trekking, canoeing, rafting, paragliding, diving – and sightseeing.
✉ **11 Karagözler, Ordu Caddesi 72, Fethiye** ☎ **0252-614 8994**
✉ **Çetin Motel Alti 1, 48340 Ölüdeniz** ☎ **0252-616 6586**

Turkish Baths
The *hamam* or Turkish bath is a tradition handed down across the millennia from ancient Rome. It started simply as a way of keeping clean, but also became one of the major social centres of any town, and it remains a place of pampered luxury. Most are open 6AM–11PM. Bathing is usually strictly segregated by sex, although a few places now offer limited hours for mixed bathing. Many upmarket hotels have their own *hamam*.

Alanya
Beyler Hamam
Single-sex and mixed baths and a full massage available.

✉ **Bostancıpınarı Caddesi 6** ☎ **0242-513 5937**

Mimoza Turkish Bath
Get scrubbed clean, hang around in the steam room, have a massage and if all that was too tiring, visit the doctor and top it all off with coffee and a snack.
✉ **Sugözü Caddesi 19** ☎ **0242-513 9193**

Antalya
Antalya Yeni Hamamı
Newly opened and spotlessly clean Turkish baths, catering largely for the tourist trade, with English- and German-speaking staff.
✉ **Sinan Mah. 1255, Sokak No. 3/A** ☎ **0242-242 5225**

Demirhan Turkish Bath
Clean and modern, with professional massage.
✉ **Güllük Caddesi** ☎ **0242-243 6196/247 5859**

Fethiye
Old Turkish Bath
Single-sex and mixed facilities available at this old *hamam* in the bazaar area. Choose between an oil massage and a soap massage, and finish with a nice cup of tea.
✉ **Hamam Sokak 2, Paspatur Bazaar** ☎ **0252-614 9318**

Marmaris
Armutalan
Supposedly the largest *hamam* in Marmaris, complete with jacuzzi, a swimming pool and coiffeur.
✉ **Cami Avlu quarter, by Karaca Sitesi Armullan** ☎ **0252-412 0710**

Sultan
This new *hamam*, in a modern shopping arcade, is aimed at the tourist trade. Single-sex and mixed baths, a choice of massages and a rest room serving drinks.
✉ **Talik Centre** ☎ **0252-413 6850**

Bath Etiquette
When using the Turkish Baths, undress in the *camekân* (reception area). Full nudity is not usual; wear your swimming costume or request a *peştamal* (sarong). You will also be given a towel and *takunya* (wooden clogs). The main chamber (*hararet*) is a hot steam room, with a large marble slab on which you lie during a face-, foot- and/or full body-massage, or a scrub-down with a camel-hair glove. There are private siderooms for washing down first.

What's On When

Grease Wrestling

Yağlı güreş (grease wrestling) is one of Turkey's most bizarre local activities, with bouts held most Sundays throughout the summer. Competitors smear themselves with oil before getting to grips with each other. Venues (usually open fields just outside town) are published in the local papers, with activities kicking off at around 11AM and the serious competition starting at around 12:30.

January/February

Camel-wrestling matches sometimes held in the Demre area (although these are more common in the Aegean region).

May

Silifke Music and Folkore Festival.

May/June

Annual international beach volley championship, Cleopatra Beach, Alanya: an event kicked off by the 1996 World Cup Beach Volley Championship, which attracted 42 teams from 24 countries.

June

Aspendos Opera and Ballet Festival: huge crowds attend a programme of performances in the magnificent ancient theatre, which attracts big names such as Pavarotti and Montserrat Caballé
Finike Festival.

July

International Folk Festival, held in Antalya and Aspendos.
Manavgat Tourism Festival; İskenderun Tourism and Culture Festival: minor festivals started to try to give a tourism focus to the area's less attractive destinations.

Summer

Grease wrestling (see panel).

September

Kemer Carnival.
Mersin International Fair.

September/October

Mersin Art and Culture Festival.

October

Altın Portakal (Golden Orange) Film Festival, Antalya: operates back-to-back with the International Akdeniz Song Competition. Both also have events at Aspendos.
Alanya Triathlon: a growing event, including several hundred competitors in a gruelling endurance/speed test, which involves swimming, cycling and running.
International Swimming Marathon, Alanya.

Moveable Festivals

Turkey celebrates three main Muslim festivals each year. All three are moveable. Ramazan (known elsewhere as Ramadan) is the month-long fast which is a basic duty of all true Muslims. Between the hours of sunrise and sunset people must abstain from sexual relations, and no food, water or tobacco must pass the lips (except for the pregnant or infirm). Otherwise, life theoretically goes on as usual. Tourist restaurants remain open, but it is best to be discreet about eating in public. Dusk every evening sees the start of a huge meal. At the end of Ramazan, Şeker Bayramı (the Candy Festival) is a three-day celebration of the end of the fast, marked with street parties and the giving and consumption of huge numbers of sweets and pastries. Kurban Bayramı, the more sombre four-day Feast of the Sacrifice, celebrates Abraham's willingness to sacrifice his son Isaac to God. Traditionally, lamb's meat is distributed among the poor.

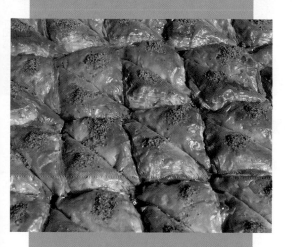

Practical Matters

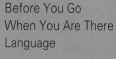

Above: *turkish pastry - a delicious oriental sweet*
Right: *old habits die hard in the countryside...*

TIME DIFFERENCES

GMT
12 noon

Turkey
2PM

Germany
1PM

USA (NY)
7AM

Netherlands
1PM

Spain
1PM

BEFORE YOU GO

WHAT YOU NEED

- ● Required
- ○ Suggested
- ▲ Not required

	UK	Germany	USA	Netherlands	Spain
Passport/National Identity Card	●	●	●	●	●
Visa (obtainable upon arrival)	●	▲	●	●	●
Onward or Return Ticket	○	○	○	○	○
Health Inoculations	▲	▲	▲	▲	▲
Health Documentation	▲	▲	▲	▲	▲
Travel Insurance	○	○	○	○	○
Driving Licence (EU or International)	●	●	●	●	●
Car Insurance Certificate (if own car)	●	●	●	●	●
Car registration document (if own car)	●	●	●	●	●

WHEN TO GO

Antalya

High season

Low season

JAN	FEB	MAR	APR	MAY	JUN	JUL	AUG	SEP	OCT	NOV	DEC
10°C	11°C	13°C	16°C	20°C	25°C	28°C	28°C	25°C	20°C	15°C	12°C

 Very wet   Wet   Cloud   Sun   Sun/Showers

TOURIST OFFICES

In the UK
Turkish Information Office
1st Floor,
Egyptian House,
170-73 Piccadilly,
London
W1V 9DD
☎ 0171-629 7771

In the USA
821 United Nations Plaza,
New York, NY 10017
☎ 212-687 2194/5

Web-site
http://www.turkey.org/
turkey

1717 Massachusetts Ave
NW,
Suite 306,
Washington, DC 20036
☎ 202-429 9844/9409

EMERGENCY (Inc. Ambulance) 112

FIRE 110

POLICE (*Polis*) – in town 155

(*Jandarma*) – in country 156   TRAFFIC POLICE 154

WHEN YOU ARE THERE

ARRIVING

Turkish Airlines has connecting scheduled services via Istanbul to Dalaman, Antalya and Adana. Onur Air and Istanbul Airlines also offer scheduled domestic services and direct international flights in summer. In high season, there are charter flights from across Europe.

Dalaman Airport Kilometres to city centre	Journey times
15 kilometres	🚆 N/A
	🚌 15 minutes
	🚗 15 minutes

Dalaman Airport Kilometres to Fethiye	Journey times
 **50 kilometres**	🚆 N/A
	🚌 N/A
	🚗 Car to Fethiye 1½ hr

MONEY

Turkey's currency is the lira (TL). The coinage is 5,000, 10,000, 25,000 and 50,000 lira pieces. The notes are 50,000TL, 100,000TL, 250,000TL, 500,000TL, 1,000,000TL and 5,000,000TL. Coins are almost worthless and are rarely used. Travellers' cheques and Eurocheques are changeable at banks and post offices. Credit cards are theoretically widely accepted but there may be problems getting authorisation. Many sales outlets prefer payment in Deutschmarks, US dollars or sterling. Rural Turkey still operates a mainly cash economy.

TIME

 Turkey is two hours ahead of GMT, and operates a summertime from late March to late October when clocks are put forward one hour.

CUSTOMS

 YES

Goods Obtained Duty Free taken into Turkey
(Limits):
Wine or spirits: 5l
Cigarettes: 200
Cigars: 50
Chocolate: 1kg; sweets: 1kg
Coffee:1.5kg
Instant coffee: 1.5kg instant
Tea: 500gm
Tobacco: 200gm
Perfume: 5 bottles (each 120ml max)
Toilet water: no limit

You are also officially allowed to take one camera with 5 rolls of film, one video camera with 5 blank video cassettes, one portable typewriter and one portable radio when you enter the country.

 NO

Drugs, firearms, ammunition, offensive weapons, obscene material, unlicensed animals. The smuggling of drugs and antiquities both carry extremely severe penalties. If buying antiques or carpets, get a clearance certificate from a museum before leaving the country.

UK
0312-468 6230

Germany
0312-426 5465

USA
0312-468 6110

Netherlands
0312-446 0470

Spain
0312-440 2169

WHEN YOU ARE THERE

TOURIST OFFICES

- Adana
  Regional Directorate,
  Çinarlı Mah, Atatürk Cad 13
  ☎ 0322-363 1287

- Alanya
  Damlataş Mağarası Yanı,
  Damlataş Cad 1
  ☎ 0242-513 1240

- Anamur
  Otogar Binası Kat 2
  ☎ 0324-814 3529

- Antalya
  TRT Binası Yanı, Tonguç
  Cad
  ☎ 0242-343 2760/1

- Cappadocia
  Atatürk Bulv, Devlet
  Hastanesi Önü, Nevşehir
  ☎ 0384-213 3659/9604

- Fethiye
  İskele Karşası 1
  ☎ 0252-614 1527

- Kaş
  Cumhuriyet Meydanı 5
  ☎ 0242-836 1238

- Kemer
  Belediye ve Turizm Binası
  ☎ 0242-814 1112

- Marmaris
  İskele Meydanı 2
  ☎ 0252-412 1035

- Side
  Side Yoly Üzeri, Manavgat
  ☎ 0242-753 1265

- Silifke
  Gazi Mah, Veli Gürten
  Bozbey Cad 6
  ☎ 0324-714 1151

NATIONAL HOLIDAYS

J	F	M	A	M	J	J	A	S	O	N	D
1	(1)	1(3)	1				1		1		

1 Jan	New Year's Day
23 Apr	National Independence and Children's Day
19 May	Atatürk Commemoration and Youth and Sports Day
30 Aug	Victory Day
29 Oct	Republic Day

Moveable Holidays
Şeker Bayramı: 3-day Candy Festival to celebrate the end of the month-long Muslim fast of Ramazan. Kurban Bayramı: 4-day Feast of the Sacrifice: lamb's meat is distributed to the poor. Both these holidays and Ramazan move backwards by 11 days each year. Şeker Bayramı will be in Feb/Jan and Kurban Bayramı in Apr/Mar until 2000.

OPENING HOURS

○ Shops   ● Post Offices
● Offices   ● Museums/Monuments
● Banks   ● Pharmacies

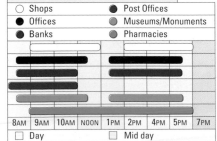

| 8AM | 9AM | 10AM | NOON | 1PM | 2PM | 4PM | 5PM | 7PM |

□ Day   □ Mid day
□ Evening

All opening times are variable. Markets open from Monday to Saturday (some on Sundays, too), 9–7. Major post offices also open Sundays, 9–7; minor post offices open during the week, 8:30–12:30 and 1:30–5:30. Many archaeological sites have open access; those with formal opening hours tend to open daily, 8:30–6. Many petrol stations open 24 hours a day, seven days a week. Some banks are open daily in the major resorts; others close at weekends. Shops and pharmacies close on Sundays; museums on Mondays.

DRIVE ON THE RIGHT

TOILETS CHARGE

PUBLIC TRANSPORT

Internal Flights Domestic flights connect with most of the major regional centres.

Trains There are some trains north to Ankara and Istanbul but there is no connecting route along the coast. Intercity coaches operate between the main bus stations of each town. Several companies may operate on the same route and do not have integrated pricing or timetables.

Buses Buses are the most popular and practical means of getting around. Fares are inexpensive and the service is usually very reliable and professional. Tickets can be purchased at the bus station (*otogar*), in advance, and sometimes on the actual bus if you board after the starting point. Smoking is not allowed on buses.

Boat Trips Turkish Maritime Lines operate ferries between Fethiye and Ródos (Rhodes); from Alanya and Taşucu to Girne (Kyrenia) and from Mersin to Mağosa (Famagusta) in Turkish Cyprus.

Dolmuş/minibus In towns and over shorter rural journeys, there is an extensive network of *dolmuş* or shared minibus taxis, which pick up and set down at any convenient place along the set route. Stand beside the road and flag one down; you pay according to distance travelled. Although very crowded, they are cheap and frequent.

DRIVING

Speed limit on motorways (*otoyol*): **120 kph**.

Speed limit on open roads: **90 kph** for cars.

Speed limit in urban areas: **50 kph**.

Seat belts must be worn in the front seat and in the rear if they are fitted.

There is a total ban on alcohol when driving.

Fuel is available as Super, Normal, and Unleaded petrol (gas) and Diesel. 24hr petrol stations are plentiful on all major roads. All are full service, have hygienic toilets and some have shops and even cafés. Price variations are narrow.

The policies of some British motoring organisations include reciprocal arrangements with the TTOK – Turkish Touring and Automobile Club (Antalya office ☎ 0242-247 0699; Mersin office, ☎ 0324-232 1247; emergency national breakdown ☎ 0212-280 4449). If the car is hired, follow the instructions given in the documentation. All accidents must be reported to the police.

CAR RENTAL

International car rental companies are all widely represented, with offices in the airports and at major towns and resorts. There are also many local firms. Advance booking is essential at peak periods and usually cost effective.

TAXIS

Yellow taxis are to be found on almost every street corner of every town. If the roof light is on, they are available for hire. Hotels and restaurants will call a cab if there is no convenient rank. All taxis have meters and reasonable, set tariffs.

At the top is a ruler showing CENTIMETRES (0–8) and INCHES (0–3).

PERSONAL SAFETY

The crime rate in Turkey is very low. Do not leave valuables lying around, carry too much visible cash, or walk down side alleys alone at night. Only the most Westernised Turkish women visit restaurants and bars, or socialise with men outside the home. If you are badly hassled, appeal to the crowd. In towns, there are general police, traffic police and, in major resorts, tourist police who speak some English, German and Arabic. In rural areas, policing is handled by the paramilitary jandarma, a branch of the army.

Police assistance:
☎ **155**
from any call box

TELEPHONES

There are pay phones on many streets, and at PTT offices, where you can also buy the *jetons* (tokens) or phone cards needed to use them. Some also accept credit cards. The phone system is slow and overloaded and many Turks use mobiles instead.

International Dialling Codes From Turkey to:	
UK:	00 44
Germany:	00 49
USA & Canada:	00 1
Netherlands:	00 31
Spain:	00 34

POST

Post offices (*postane*) are recognisable by their large yellow signs with PTT written in black. All major post offices operate *poste restante*, have foreign exchange desks and have public phones. Stamps are available from post offices, and from some sweet and souvenir shops and hotels.

ELECTRICITY

220V AC. Sockets accept standard continental two-pin plugs. Visitors from the UK

require an adaptor and US visitors a voltage transformer.
Power cuts are frequent but short-lived in winter.

TIPS/GRATUITIES

Yes ✓ No ✗		
Restaurants (service included)	✓	10%
Cafés/Bar (service not inc.)	✓	small change
Taxis	✓	round up
Tour guides	✓	10–15%
Porters	✓	100–250,000TL
Chambermaids	✓	100–250,000TL
Toilets	✓	30–50,000TL
Masseurs/masseuses	✓	100–250,000TL
Shoe attendants in mosques	✓	small change

What to photograph: everything. Turkey is immensely photogenic.
What not to photograph: always ask permission before photographing people. Strict Muslims may refuse, but many are delighted. Do not take photos of any military or police personnel or structure.
When to photograph: the midday sun is strong, the light flat and the shadows harsh. The best light for photography is in the early mornings and late afternoon.
Where to buy film: larger towns have photographic shops.

HEALTH

Insurance
All travellers are strongly advised to take out comprehensive travel insurance with good medical cover. There are no reciprocal health agreements.

Dental Services
Dental treatment must be paid for. Check your travel insurance to see whether, and to what extent, dental treatment is covered.

Sun Advice
Avoid the midday sun: sunbathing should be rationed to prevent sunburn, heatstroke and longer-term skin damage. Use a high factor sunblock.

Drugs
Pharmacies (*eczane*) are plentiful and are a good first stop for treatment. Pharmacists routinely diagnose and treat minor conditions while many drugs, including antibiotics, which are only sold with a prescription in western Europe or the USA are available over the counter. Hotels, tourist boards, tour operators' reps, consulates and pharmacists can recommend a good English-speaking doctor or state clinic. The private hospitals are generally good, clean and efficient.

Food and Water
The most likely ailment is simple diarrhoea, brought on by mild food poisoning, heatstroke or alcohol abuse (or a combination of all three). Avoid tap water: bottled mineral water is widely available. Avoid food that has been standing around in the open for any length of time.

CONCESSIONS

There are some concessions on entrances to students with an International Student Identity Card (ISIC), and passengers with disabilities get a substantial discount on the trains. In general, however, the discounts are few and far between and prices are not sufficiently high to make the time spent chasing them cost-effective.

CLOTHING SIZES

Turkey	UK	Rest of Europe	USA		
46	36	46	36		
48	38	48	38		
50	40	50	40		
52	42	52	42		Suits
54	44	54	44		
56	46	56	46		
41	7	41	8		
42	7.5	42	8.5		
43	8.5	43	9.5		
44	9.5	44	10.5		Shoes
45	10.5	45	11.5		
46	11	46	12		
37	14.5	37	14.5		
38	15	38	15		
39/40	15.5	39/40	15.5		
41	16	41	16		Shirts
42	16.5	42	16.5		
43	17	43	17		
36	8	34	6		
38	10	36	8		
40	12	38	10		
42	14	40	12		Dresses
44	16	42	14		
46	18	44	16		
38	4.5	38	6		
38	5	38	6.5		
39	5.5	39	7		
39	6	39	7.5		Shoes
40	6.5	40	8		
41	7	41	8.5		

WHEN DEPARTING

- Reconfirm your flight 72 hours before you leave.
- Contact the airline/airport on the day before departure to ensure that flight details are unchanged.
- Keep exchange receipts, sales slips and VAT vouchers in your hand luggage if you wish to re-exchange money or claim tax back on any purchases.

LANGUAGE

Turkish, loosely related to Finnish and Hungarian, is an extremely difficult language that builds sentences by adding extra syllables to the basic word, rather than using verbs. The addition of a suffix can also alter the structure of the basic word and make it virtually unrecognisable to the untrained eye. Use a phrase book and keep it simple. Pronunciation ai/ay long i, eg side; c a hard j, eg jam; ç ch, eg chat; ı er/uh, eg letter; ğ y; ü ew, eg few (roughly); ö ur (more like the Scandinanvian ø); j zh (no English equivalent); ş sh, eg shut.

hotel	hotel/otel	with a sea view	deniz manzaralı
bed and breakfast	pansiyon	balcony	balkon
do you have a		lift	asansör
room?	boş odanız var mi?	room service	oda servisi
single/double/	tek/çift/üç kişilik	air conditioning	havalandırma
triple		central heating	kalorifer
I have a reser-	reservasyonım var	hot water	sicak su
vation		bath	banyo
bank	banka	expensive	pahalı
exchange office	kamiyo büroso	what is the	fıatı nedir?
post office	postane	price?	
travellers'	seyahat çeki	ten	on
cheque		fifty	elli
credit card	kredi kartı	one hundred	yüz
exchange rate	dövis kuru	two hundred	ikiyüz
how much?	ne kadar?	one thousand	bin
I'd like a table for	iki kişilik bir	vegetarian	etsiz yemekler
two	masa	dishes	
waiter	garson	bread	ekmek
menu	menü	beer	bira
soup	çorba	red/white wine	kırmızı/beyaz
fish	balık		şarap
meat dishes	etli yemekler	bill	hesap
fruit	meyva	service included	servis hariç
aeroplane	uçak	car	araba
airport	havaalanı	petrol	benzin
train	tren		(super/normal)
railway station	tren ıstasyonu	boat	gemi
bus	otobus	ferry	vapur/feribot
bus stop	emanet	port/harbour	liman
bus station	otogar	ticket	bilet
taxi	taksi	single/return	gidiş/gidiş dönüş
hello	merhaba	you're welcome	bir şey değil
goodbye	allaha ısmarladik	I don't under-	sizi anlamiyorum
	(person going)	stand	
goodbye	güle güle (person	do you speak	İngilizce
	staying)	English?	konuşmasını
yes	evet		biliyor
no	hayir/yok		musunuz?
please	lütfen	open	açik
thank you	teşekkür	closed	kapalı
	ederim/mersi	leave me alone	beni rahat bırat

INDEX

Acknowledgements
The Automobile Association wishes to thank the following photographers and libraries for their
assistance in the preparation of this book.
AKG LONDON 10b (Erich Lessing); THE J ALLAN CASH PHOTOLIBRARY 62, 79; ART DIRECTORS/
TRIP PHOTO LIBRARY 90b (M Jenkin); BRUCE COLEMAN COLLECTION 12b; ROBERT HARDING
PICTURE LIBRARY 46, 47, 63; PICTURES COLOUR LIBRARY 92; POWERSTOCK/ZEFA F/Cover c
(Woman in traditional costume); M SHALES 40b, 41, 61, 78b, 91b; SPECTRUM COLOUR LIBRARY
23b. All remaining pictures are held in the Association's own library (AA PHOTO LIBRARY) and were
taken by Jean François Pin with exception of the following: P Kenward F/Cover b (gulet), 8c, 13a, 15a,
16a, 16b, 17a, 18a, 18b, 19a, 20a, 21a, 22a, 23a, 24a, 24b, 24/5, 25a, 25b, 26a, 26b, 28/9, 31b, 32b,
32/3, 34a, 34b, 35b, 37, 43a, 44, 49, 51b, 52, 53a, 54a, 54b, 56a, 57a, 58a, 60a, 64a, 65a, 65b, 66/7,
68a, 70a, 71b, 72, 74, 76b, 77, 81, 84, 89, 117a, 122c; D Mitideri 2, 9c, 27b, 42, 51a, 68c, 69, 88; T
Souter 50.

Author's Acknowledgements
The author would like to thank the following people and organisations for their generous assistance
during the researching of this book: Dwynwen Berry, for driving long hours on perilous roads; Wanda
Etheridge in Tarsus, Brigitta Dikmen in Kemer, and Mustafa Aydın and Ferhat Malcan in Kaş for
invaluable information; Peter Espley of the Turkish Tourist Office in London; Sarah Moy of the
Marketing Machine, Sunquest Holidays, Sheraton Hotels, the Hotel Club Green Fugla Beach,
İnçekum, and the Sultan Saray Hotel, Kemer for assistance with accommodation.

Copy editor: Nia Williams   Page Layout: Design 23

Dear Essential Traveller

**Your comments, opinions and recommendations are very
important to us. So please help us to improve our travel
guides by taking a few minutes to complete this simple
questionnaire.**

*You do not need a stamp (unless posted outside the UK). If you do not want to cut this page
from your guide, then photocopy it or write your answers on a plain sheet of paper.*

Send to: **The Editor, AA World Travel Guides,
FREEPOST SCE 4598, Basingstoke RG21 4GY.**

Your recommendations...

We always encourage readers' recommendations for restaurants, nightlife
or shopping – if your recommendation is used in the next edition of the
guide, we will send you a *FREE* AA *Essential* **Guide** of your choice.
Please state below the establishment name, location and your reasons
for recommending it.

_____

_____

_____

_____

Please send me **AA *Essential*** _____

(*see list of titles inside the front cover*)

About this guide...

Which title did you buy?

AA *Essential* _____

Where did you buy it? _____

When? m m / y y

Why did you choose an AA *Essential* Guide? _____

_____

_____

_____

_____

Did this guide meet your expectations?

Exceeded ☐   Met all ☐   Met most ☐   Fell below ☐

Please give your reasons _____

_____

_____

_____

continued on next page...

Were there any aspects of this guide that you particularly liked? _____

_____

_____

_____

Is there anything we could have done better? _____

_____

_____

_____

_____

About you…

Name (*Mr/Mrs/Ms*) _____

Address _____

_____ Postcode _____

Daytime tel nos _____

Which age group are you in?
Under 25 ☐ 25–34 ☐ 35–44 ☐ 45–54 ☐ 55–64 ☐ 65+ ☐

How many trips do you make a year?
Less than one ☐ One ☐ Two ☐ Three or more ☐

Are you an AA member? Yes ☐ No ☐

About your trip…

When did you book? m m / y y   When did you travel? m m / y y
How long did you stay? _____
Was it for business or leisure? _____
Did you buy any other travel guides for your trip?
If yes, which ones? _____

_____

Thank you for taking the time to complete this questionnaire. Please send
it to us as soon as possible, and remember, you do not need a stamp
(*unless posted outside the UK*).

Happy Holidays!